Mison 美森教育

丛书主编◎孙乐

剑桥领思备考
强化系列

Linguaskill

Linguaskill
50天攻克
剑桥领思 通用英语

写作篇:9天
WRITING

编著◎陈亦馨

大连理工大学出版社
Dalian University of Technology Press

图书在版编目（CIP）数据

50天攻克剑桥领思通用英语. 写作篇. 9天 / 陈亦馨
编著. -- 大连：大连理工大学出版社，2023.12
（剑桥领思备考强化系列丛书 / 孙乐主编）
ISBN 978-7-5685-4658-4

Ⅰ. ①5⋯ Ⅱ. ①陈⋯ Ⅲ. ①英语水平考试—写作—
自学参考资料 Ⅳ. ①H310.41

中国国家版本馆CIP数据核字（2023）第197422号

大连理工大学出版社出版
地址：大连市软件园路80号　邮政编码：116023
发行：0411-84708842　邮购：0411-84708943　传真：0411-84701466
E-mail：dutp@dutp.cn　　　　URL：https://www.dutp.cn/
辽宁星海彩色印刷有限公司印刷　　　大连理工大学出版社发行

幅面尺寸：185mm×260mm　　印张：16　　　字数：370千字
2023年12月第1版　　　　　　　2023年12月第1次印刷

责任编辑：李玉霞　张晓燕　　　　　　责任校对：钟　宇
封面设计：美森教育

ISBN 978-7-5685-4658-4　　　　　定　价：60.00元

本书如有印装质量问题，请与我社发行部联系更换。

前　言

一、剑桥领思考试简介

剑桥领思（Linguaskill）是由英国剑桥大学英语考评部研发的一项在线英语测评，它借助人工智能技术来测试应试者的英语水平。剑桥领思以模块的形式，全面测试听、说、读、写四项英语技能。剑桥领思的特点是快速便捷，由于是在线考试，考生可以随时随地参加。同时，相比于传统考试，剑桥领思可以快速提供成绩，一般在考试完成后72 小时内考生就可以获得成绩报告。考试成绩对标欧洲语言共同参考框架（CEFR），该框架是描述学习者语言能力的国际标准。由于其高效、准确、权威，目前剑桥领思已获得数千家国际组织机构的认可，在中国，认可剑桥领思成绩的组织机构包括但不限于中国石油天然气集团、中建国际建设、中国五矿集团、美的集团、中山华利集团、中国教育国际交流协会、山东省人民政府外事办公室、西交利物浦大学、宁波诺丁汉大学、昆山杜克大学等。

根据考生自身目标和想测试的英语种类，剑桥领思考试分为剑桥领思通用英语测评和剑桥领思职场英语测评两种。其中，剑桥领思通用英语测评更侧重日常生活与学习等英语应用语境，测试的是日常生活英语。

二、本套书编写目的

目前市面上针对剑桥领思通用英语的备考书籍几乎处于空白，想要参加这一考试的考生急需相关的学习材料。美森教育图书编撰委员会的教师为了满足广大考生的这一需求，编写了本套图书。希望本套图书能成为众多考生领思通用英语备考路上的得力助手，帮助大家获得高分。

三、本套书核心特色

1. 以题型为主线，循序渐进提升

本套书包含听力篇、阅读篇、写作篇和口语篇4个分册，每个分册都是以考试题型为主线来编排的，考生在学习时可以逐个题型一一突破，稳扎稳打。在内容上，本套书

非常注重知识的循序渐进，每个题型的学习都按照"基础篇—提分篇—实战篇"来设置，考生先通过"基础篇"掌握每种题型考查的内容和基本的答题策略，然后通过"提分篇"来深入学习重点、难点，最后通过"实战篇"来做题巩固。这一结构安排可以让考生将每种题型吃透，对知识的掌握也会更牢固。

2. 精选高质量的实战习题，充分练习

本书编写团队的教师均是剑桥领思中国运营中心的合作教师，且一线教学经验丰富。本套书中的所有实战习题也都是在总结大量领思通用英语考试试题后编写而成的，与真实考试的考点、难度高度一致，对于考生来说是非常宝贵的练习材料，考生一定要充分练习，多进行总结，实现稳步提升。

3. 提供详细解析，厘清解题思路

无论任何考试，相信考生都清楚一点：做题重要，总结更重要。因此，本套书中的所有习题均提供了详细的解析，为考生梳理解题思路。考生在做完题后要仔细研读解析，总结每道题的考点、自己理解有误之处以及未掌握的知识点，有针对性地查缺补漏。

4. 全真模拟题，考前冲刺提升

本套书每个分册的最后一章都提供了全真模拟题，让考生在考前进行模拟练习，做最后的冲刺提升。每套全真模拟题都力求还原真实考试，考生可以检验自己的学习成果，之后对于不足再次进行强化训练。

5. 英籍外教原声音频，扫码即听

本套书听力分册的音频由英籍外教录音，发音纯正，语音、语调、停顿等细节也充分还原真实考试。书中提供了二维码，扫码即可获取音频，方便考生随时随地听音。

在筹备及编写本套书的过程中，美森教育图书编撰委员会以下资深教师委员也参与了工作，他们分别是：孙乐、孙旭、李建荣、姚宝娇、杨李健、陈雪、孙晓丹、于京圣、姚宝丹、邢思毅、隋良东、景作鹏、皮姗姗、邢汝国、景文学、隋秀丽、景文菊、陈威、刘庆杰、孙连军、宋海蛟、周翼、潘宇、尹辉、张清川、孙成伟、辛连厚、吴馨玲、邵淑梅、侯殿东、朱汉民、王守斌、韩琦、崔林杰、杨丹、王海军等，在此一并表示感谢。

希望本套书能够切实地帮助到广大的领思考生，同时也真诚期待热心的读者对本书提出宝贵的意见和建议。

美森教育

www.mison.cn

关注"剑桥领思考试"微信公众号
随时随地获取领思学习干货

致读者

亲爱的本书读者：

在您正式开始学习本书之前，请务必扫描下面的二维码观看本书的使用讲解视频，同时获取读者专享免费课程。

视频是本书作者团队的代表教师特意录制的，为大家介绍了本书的特点和结构，并精讲了高效使用本书的具体方法。

读者专享免费课程是给大家额外附赠的领思通用英语备考课（价值599元），该课程适用于所有备考领思通用英语的考生，为大家详细讲解备考重点，提供考试指导。

相信大家在看过视频和课程之后，能够有效提高学习效率，最终获得领思高分。

目　录

Part 2　长文本

考前冲刺——全真模拟题

参考范文与翻译

带你认识剑桥领思写作考试

一、剑桥领思通用英语测评概述

1. 剑桥领思通用英语测评简介

剑桥领思（Linguaskill）是2020年由剑桥英语考评部（Cambridge English Assessment）推出的一项权威、快速、便捷的在线英语水平测试，应试者可以通过该测试了解自己的英语听、说、读、写水平。

该测试具有以下几个特点：

（1）便捷。可以在考生熟悉的场地、方便的时间安排测试，并通过电脑与手机联网进行远程监考。

（2）模块化考试。考生可以根据需要评估的能力，自由选择各测试模块。目前共分为三个模块，分别是阅读和听力（Reading and Listening）、写作（Writing）和口语（Speaking）。

（3）成绩准确。阅读及听力模块以人工智能为支撑，采用最先进的自适应性理论，试题的难易程度会依据应试者对前一个问题的回答情况而调整。

（4）出分快。通常可以在考试后72小时内获得成绩报告。

模块构成：

测试项目	测试时长
阅读和听力（二合一）	60~85分钟
写作	45分钟
口语	15分钟

根据考生自身英语测评目标和想测试的英语种类，考试分为剑桥领思通用英语测评和剑桥领思职场英语测评两种。剑桥领思通用更侧重日常生活与学习等英语应用环境，测试的是日常生活英语。考试话题包括学习和工作、制订未来计划、旅行和技术等等。

剑桥领思通用英语测评的特点在于它是一项侧重能力并且涉及主题广泛的考试，考试的材料多与日常生活、学习相关，因此对日常生活各项主题与词汇的把握是考生获得高分的一个重要因素。剑桥领思通用英语测评的用词较为日常化，单词含义也较为简单，但涉及的话题较为宽泛，需要考生多积累相关常识与词汇。

2. 剑桥领思考试流程

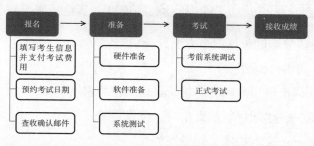

二、写作考试概述

写作模块由两部分构成，答题时间共45分钟。第一部分，考生阅读一篇短消息，通常是一封邮件，然后根据消息中的信息和给出的三个要点写一篇不少于50个单词的邮件。答题时长为15分钟。第二部分，考生阅读一段概述某情境的短文，然后根据情境中的信息和写作要求中给出的三个要点作答。考生需要写出一篇不少于180个单词的小短文、评论、信件、意见、邮件或者帖子。答题时长为30分钟。两部分分别占写作成绩总分的一半。

三、写作考试题型介绍

写作模块一共包括两部分，第一部分是根据提供的邮件以及题目后面提出的要点写一篇不少于50个单词的邮件；第二部分是写一篇不少于180个单词的小短文、评论、信件、意见、邮件或者帖子。

这里要强调一点，小作文的分值占整个写作成绩的一半，也就是说小作文和大作文一样重要。大作文要求写一篇小短文、评论、信件、意见、邮件或者帖子。需要注意，这里不要求写议论文，即无需进行正反论述，无需进行辩证思考，无需使用总分总的写作结构，而是要求就事论事，体现阐述自我意见的能力即可。

项目	部分	题型	时间	具体内容
写作	1	电子邮件	15分钟	根据提供的邮件以及题目后面提出的要点写一篇不少于50个单词的邮件
	2	长文本	30分钟	阅读一篇概述某情境的短文，然后根据情境中的信息和给出的三个要点写一篇小短文、评论、信件、意见、邮件或者帖子

四、写作考试评分标准与成绩解读

写作考试的评分维度包括四个方面，分别是：

➤ 词汇——单词、词组

➤ 语法——词汇使用准确性、句子表达的精练程度

➤ 书写规则——单词拼写、大小写、标点符号

➤ 观点拓展——文章长度、句子连贯性

结合官方范文可发现，除内容外，最直观的一个得分点就是字数，所以推荐大家尽量多写，保证内容的多样性和丰富性是取得高分的一个关键因素。除此之外，作文对词汇量的要求不是很高，所以，考生要在保证用词准确、拼写无误的前提下，尽可能多地丰富内容和观点，不必纠结各种长难复杂句式的运用。写出完整切题、符合题目各个要点的内容就能拿到高分。

剑桥领思通过使用CEFR欧标来评测考生的真实英文能力，采用分段方式（82~180+）来报告成绩，同时提供从"A1及以下"到"C1及以上"多个级别来反馈考生的英语水平，成绩报告单样式如下：

Linguaskill ▶▶

Institution
Username
Ref. No.

Test Report

Linguaskill General

Candidate name

Candidate number

Date of birth

Organisation

Average Score	139	CEFR Level	A2

→ 总分和总级别

Below A1	**A1**	**A2**	**B1**	**B2**	**C1 or above**

Skill	Test Date	Score	CEFR Level
Listening	14 July 2022	126	A2

→ 单项分和单项的级别

Below A1	A1	A2	B1	B2	C1 or above

每个单项分数对应的英语能力描述，考生可以了解自己在哪些方面表现良好，哪些方面有待提高

Can understand the main point of short, clear, sentence-length speech about daily life and work situations. Can recognise phrases and vocabulary closely related to their life, but is likely to rely on repetition, simplified speech, slow speech, or guessing to grasp meaning.

Skill	Test Date	Score	CEFR Level
Reading	14 July 2022	116	A1

Below A1	A1	A2	B1	B2	C1 or above

Can understand familiar names, words and simple sentences in very short, simple texts such as advertisements, menus, timetables and roadmaps. Re-reading is often required.

Skill	Test Date	Score	CEFR Level
Speaking	14 July 2022	157	B1

Below A1	A1	A2	B1	B2	C1 or above

Can answer questions about routine matters, connecting phrases simply to describe experiences and events and give brief reasons, explanations, reactions or opinions on familiar topics.

Skill	Test Date	Score	CEFR Level
Writing	14 July 2022	156	B1

Below A1	A1	A2	B1	B2	C1 or above

Can write straightforward, connected text on familiar topics by linking shorter elements into a sequence. Can write a description of an experience or event.

写作模块对应的分数及英语能力描述如下所示：

写作水平	剑桥领思通用英语测试成绩	英语能力描述
熟练自如	C1及以上（180+）	• 能够以适当且有效的风格和逻辑结构书写清晰、流畅、复杂的文本，有助于读者找出重点。
独立运用	B2（160~179）	• 能够针对与兴趣领域相关的各类主题撰写清晰详细的文本，并且表现出在书面文本中可以使用不同表达方式的能力。
	B1（140~159）	• 能够对感兴趣的领域中多个熟悉的主题进行简单的描写，将一系列简短分散的语言要素组合成连贯的句子。
基础能力	A2（120~139）	• 能够简单地描述个人背景、周边环境和切身需求。
	A1（100~119）	• 能够写出简单、无关联的短语和句子。
/	A1及以下（82~99）	/

考生也可以通过下表对领思成绩与其他剑桥考试的成绩进行一个直观的对比。

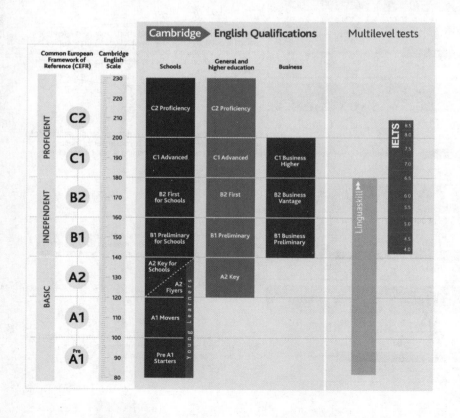

Part 1 电子邮件

Day 1   基础篇——题型介绍

一、题型简介

写作考试的第一部分首先出现的是一则简短的消息，通常是一封电子邮件。考生需仔细阅读题目和下面的要点，然后写一封不少于50个单词的回复邮件。考生有15分钟的时间来完成这一部分的写作。答题时需要以题目要求中的三个要点为依据，尽可能每一个要点多写一点内容，确保文章达到字数要求。

二、考试界面

登陆考试账号之后，首先出现的是如下所示的界面。界面中提供的信息是对考试情况的说明，考生阅读之后可以点击右下角的"Start"按钮进入正式的答题界面。

Linguaskill▶▶ General

Sample Test

Instructions and Information

The writing test lasts 45 minutes.

There are two parts to this test.

Answer both parts. You should spend about 15 minutes on Part 1 and about 30 minutes on Part 2.

Use the arrow buttons at the bottom of the screen to move between parts.

You can change your answers at any time during the test.

When you are ready click on 'Start' to continue.

Start

点击"Start"按钮后进入正式的答题页面，页面内的功能和内容介绍如下：

➤ 页面最上方的中间位置显示考试剩余时间。

➤ 页面左半部分是试题内容，考生需要根据提供的邮件、广告信息或其他内容来写邮件，具体的邮件内容、回信要求及字数要求会在试题中进行说明。

➤ 页面右半部分是答题区域，考生在此区域作答，可以使用文本框左上角的

"Cut""Copy"和"Paste"功能键对文本内容进行编辑。

➢ 文本框左下方的"Word count"处显示的是文本框内已经完成的单词数量，便于考生计算邮件包含的字数。

➢ 点击页面右下角的箭头可以对小作文和大作文的页面进行切换，切换的过程不影响答案的保存，考生可自由切换来查看完成进度。

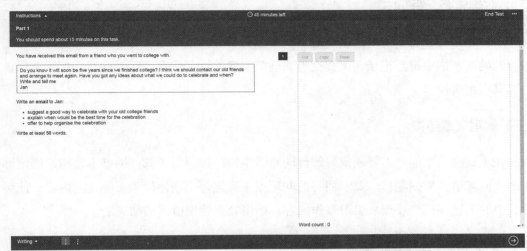

下面的界面是Part Two部分的内容，可以通过右下角的箭头对这两部分内容进行切换。

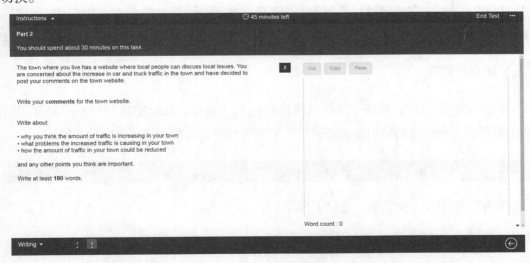

三、答题步骤

写作考试第一部分的电子邮件写作可以按照下面的步骤来进行：

(一) 阅读题目要求，明确写作内容

考生在答题前需要仔细阅读屏幕上的说明和信息，根据题目要求思考写作内容；结合要点信息明确需要提供的信息。

(二) 明确思路，组织内容

在对题目要求有了清晰的了解之后，考生可以在头脑中思考写作内容，也可以在电脑答题的文本框中进行记录，但提交答案前需要删除这些信息。思考的过程中需要保证内容具有逻辑性。

(三) 确定文章结构

在正式书写之前，需要确定好邮件的整体结构。按照电子邮件的基本结构来确定称呼语、问候语；根据题目中要求回答的问题点来确定每个主体段落要陈述的内容；使用题目中的信息和三个要点来组织写作内容；结尾处要使用恰当的结束语。

(四) 对文章进行整体输出

确定了整体结构和主体段落的内容之后，考生需要把自己的思路输出到电脑上。输出的过程中需要注意单词拼写及句子表达等语法知识点。同时需要注意对答题时间和完成字数进行把控。

(五) 提交前检查

在提交答案之前，花3~5分钟时间检查完成的邮件。检查的内容包括思路是否清晰、单词拼写和标点的使用是否正确、语法结构和字词的使用是否正确且合理等。

四、注意事项

写作过程中，考生需要注意以下事项：

(一) 注意对任务要求分别做出回复

考生在对原始邮件进行回复时，需要对题目中的每个任务要求分别进行回复。题目中通常会提出三点任务要求，考生在写作的过程中需要对这三点要求分别进行回复。

（二）注意打字速度

领思考试的形式是机考，考生需要在电脑上输出自己的答案。因此，在规定的时间内完成构思并输出不少于规定字数的作文对考生的打字速度也是一种考验。考生在平时需要多加练习，提高自己的打字速度，从而避免在考试中因为打字速度过慢而影响自己的成绩。

（三）善用考试界面提供的工具

答题文本框的左上方有三个按钮，分别是"Cut""Copy"和"Paste"，考生可以使用这几个按钮对文本框中的内容进行"剪切""复制"和"粘贴"；当然考生也可以使用快捷键Ctrl+ c/ x/ v来完成相应的操作。此外，答题文本框底部的字数统计功能可以帮助考生了解已经写了多少个单词。

（四）注意语气和词汇的使用

领思通用英语测评中涉及的题目大多与生活相关，第一部分电子邮件中涉及的内容多为同学、朋友间的信函往来，信函的内容主要为与日常生活相关的话题，因此语域特点应该为非正式文体，考生在进行这部分邮件写作时应注意词汇的表达要更贴近生活，同时需要注意表达出的语气要亲切、礼貌、客气。

（五）内容多多益善

小作文的字数要求是不少于50个单词，对字数上限没有要求，为了展现写作能力，考生应该尽量多写一些内容。而且根据多数考生的实际经验，在没有语法错误的情况下，字数越多越有利于分数的提高。

五、常用时态与从句表达

英文表达中，时态表达错误是一个常见的现象，在第一部分的邮件写作中考生同样需要注意这一问题。这部分将对常用的时态进行讲解，使考生对各种时态的运用规则有一个清晰的了解。

时态是一种动词形式，不同的时态表示不同的时间与方式。它是表示行为、动作、状态在各种时间条件下的动词形式。英语中有16种时态，下面笔者将对领思写作考试中常用到的时态进行讲解说明。

（一）一般现在时

1. 定义

一般现在时表示主语的状态、特征，经常性、反复性发生的动作或真理。

2. 用法

a. 基本用法：

➔ 表示经常性或习惯性的动作、存在的状态。

例：I often go to school by bike. 我经常骑自行车上学。

➔ 表示现在的情况或状态。

例：He is a law student. 他是一名法律系的学生。

➔ 表示客观事实或普遍真理。

例：The earth goes around the sun. 地球绕着太阳转。

b. 静态动词（表示一种状态）常用于一般现在时。

例：I love music. 我喜欢音乐。

常见的静态动词包括：

admire、concern、feel、hear、involve、require、smell、adore、consist、fit、hold、keep、matter、possess、resemble、sound、appear、contain、forget、hope、know、mean、prefer、satisfy、suppose、depend、doubt、guess、imagine、lack、need、realize、suspect、believe、deserve、impress、owe、recognize、understand、belong、desire、exist、include、own、remember、seem、wish 等等。

c. 短暂动词（表示极短暂的动作）常用于一般现在时。

例：The presenter declares this festival open. 主持人宣布庆祝活动开始。

d. 一般现在时表示将来。

➔ 用在状语从句中（如时间、条件状语从句等），用一般现在时表示将来。

例：If it rains tomorrow, we won't go to the park. 如果明天下雨，我们就不去公园了。

if引导的条件状语从句，句子时态采用"主将从现"的原则。

➔ 下列动词：come、go、arrive、leave、start、begin、return的一般现在时可以表将来。主要用来表示已经安排好时间的事情，如：

例：The train leaves at six tomorrow morning. 火车明天早上六点开。

（二）现在进行时

1. 定义

现在进行时表示现在正在进行的动作或存在的状态。现在进行时表示动作发生的时间是"现在"，动作的状态是"正在进行中"。

2. 构成

肯定句：主语+ am/ is/ are +现在分词

否定句：主语+ am/ is/ are +not +现在分词

疑问句：Am/ Is/ Are+主语+现在分词?

疑问代词/疑问副词+ am/ is/ are +主语+现在分词?

3. 基本用法

➡ 表示说话时正在进行的动作。

常和now连用，有时和动词如look、listen等连用，表示"现在"这一概念。

例：Listen! Birds are singing. 听！鸟儿们在歌唱。

　　Look! The train is just getting into the station. 看！火车进站啦。

　　He is reading now. 他正在读书。

　　The river is flowing fast after last night's rain. 昨夜下雨后，河水流速很快。

　　The house is being painted. 房子正在粉刷中。

➡ 表示现阶段正在进行着的动作。

现阶段正在进行着的动作，不一定指说话时正在进行着的动作。常和at present（目前），this week（本周），these days（这几天）等时间状语连用。

例：We're looking for a house to rent for the summer. 我们在找一栋房子，想租一个夏天。

　　Are you trying to find a furnished house? 您是想找一栋有家具的房子吗？

　　What courses are you studying this term? 你这学期学哪几门课？

　　Don't take that ladder away. Your father's using it. 别把那个梯子拿走，你父亲在用。

➡ 表示当前的动向。

例：People are getting less tolerant of smoking these days. 如今人们对吸烟变得更难以容忍了。

　　Houses are costing more these days. 如今房价更贵了。

　　She is resembling her mother more and more as the years go by. 随着岁月的

流逝，她越来越像她母亲了。

➡ 表示事先计划好的动作（指将来）。

表示在最近按计划将进行的一个动作或为将来安排好的活动，通常需要一个表示时间的状语。

例：We are spending next summer in England. 明年夏天我们将在英国度过。

I'm getting married tomorrow. 我明天就要结婚了。

用arrive（到达）、come（到来）、go（走、离去）、leave（离开）等动词的现在进行时描述行程安排，有"将到达"和"将离去"的意思。

例：He's arriving tomorrow morning on the 7:30 train. 明天早上他将乘7时30分的火车到达。

Christmas is coming soon. 圣诞节就快到了。

I'm leaving England and going to live in Spain. 我将离开英国去西班牙定居。

➡ 表示重复的动作。

副词always（表示屡次）、repeatedly（再三地）、forever（总是、不断地）等可与进行时连用，表示不断重复的动作。

例：She's always helping people. 她经常帮助别人。

He's always causing troubles. 他总是在制造麻烦。

The little boy is forever asking questions. 这个小男孩总是没完没了地问问题。

4. 一般现在时和现在进行时的区别

一般现在时表示经常性的动作；现在进行时表示暂时性的动作。

例：—Do you ever eat meat?

—No, I never eat meat.

——你平常吃肉吗？

——不，我从不吃肉。（习惯、经常性的动作）

I'm eating meat now. 我正在吃肉。（暂时性的动作）

My brother always forgets to wash behind his ears. 我弟弟总是忘记洗他的耳后根。（经常性的动作）

➡ 现在进行时有时可代替一般现在时，表达说话人的某种感情色彩，与always、forever连用。

例：Our burglar alarm is forever going off for no reason. 我们的防盗报警器总是无故响起。（含有抱怨的意思）

You are always forgetting the important thing. 你总是把重要的事情忘掉。（表

达不满情绪）

How are you feeling today? 你今天感觉怎样？（比 How do you feel today? 显得更亲切些。）

（三）现在完成时

1. 定义

现在完成时主要有两个含义：

（1）表示动作发生在过去，但与现在的情况有联系，有时无时间状语，有时和一些表示不确定的过去时间状语连用，如：many times、just、yet、ever、never、already、before、so far、by now等。

（2）表示从过去某一时间开始一直延续到现在并且还可能继续延续下去的动作，用于延续性动词，且句中常带有表示一段时间的时间状语，如：for two months、so far等。

2. 构成

主语+have/ has +动词过去分词

3. 基本用法

➜ 表示截止到现在已完成的动作。

例：By now, I have collected all the data that I need. 到现在为止，我已收集到了我所需的全部资料。

She has read 150 pages today. 她今天已看了150页。

We haven't met for many years. 我们已多年没见了。

They have developed a new product. 他们已经研制了一种新产品。

➜ 表示发生在过去而对现在产生影响、带来结果的动作。

例：Have you had your dinner? 你吃晚饭了吗？

She has been to the United States. 她已经去美国了。

You have grown much taller. 你长高了许多。

➜ 表示过去发生的动作持续到现在，并可能延续下去。

例：It has been five years since he joined the army. 他参军已经五年了。

They have learned English for eight years. 他们已学了八年的英语了。

So far we've only discussed the first five chapters. 至今我们还只讨论了前五章。

4. 现在完成时的时间状语

➜ 在使用现在完成时的句子里，不可以带有表示具体过去时间的状语，如：yester-day、last week、two weeks ago、in 1999等；现在完成时常和一些副词连用，如：just、 before、already、often、never、ever、not yet、always等。

➡ 在以when提问的特殊疑问句中不能用现在完成时。另外，ago不能用于现在完成时，因为它表示从现在算起的以前某个时间，属于表示具体过去时间的状语。但是可以用before来表示"以前"的意义，因为它只表示"以前"，而不指具体多长时间的以前。

➡ 如果将不表示连续性的动词用于现在完成时的句子，不可以与用for引导的表"一段时间"的状语连用。在这种情况下，应该用"It has been...since..."的句式来表达。如：

例：He has joined the army for five years.（错误）

It has been five years since he joined the army.（正确）

（四）一般过去时

1. 定义

一般过去时指的是过去发生的动作或存在的状态。

2. 构成

➡ 含有Be动词的一般过去时

肯定句式：主语 + be（was/ were）+ 其他

否定句式：主语 + be（was/ were）+ not + 其他

➡ 实义动词的一般过去时

肯定句要使用动词的过去式，否定句和疑问句要使用助动词didn't（did not = didn't）和did。

肯定句式：主语 + 动词（过去式）+ 其他。

否定句式：主语 + didn't + 动词（原形）+ 其他

3. 基本用法

➡ 表示在过去某个时间所发生的动作或所处的状态（与现在无关）。常与yesterday、last week、in 1989、 just now、a moment ago、the other day等表示过去具体时间的状语连用。

例：I got to know her in 2001. 我是2001年认识她的。

My grandfather died last year. 我祖父是去年去世的。

She suffered a lot in her childhood. 小时候她受了很多苦。

He believed that he was right. 他相信自己是对的。

➡ 表示在过去一段时间内的经常性或习惯性的动作。

例：We often played together when we were children. 我们小时候常在一起玩。

注：表示过去经常发生的动作还可用used to 和would

例：He used to smoke a lot, but he doesn't now. 他过去经常抽烟，但现在不抽了。

Whenever we were in trouble, he would help us. 每当我们遇到困难，他都会帮助我们。

➡ 表示主语过去的特征或性格。

例：At that time she was very good at English. 那时她英语很好。

➡ 一般过去时有时可以表示现在，多与 want、hope、wonder、think、intend 等动词连用，使语气更委婉。

例：I wondered if you could help me. 我不知道你能不能帮我。

➡ 有时用一般过去时也是时态一致的需要。

例：I didn't know you were here. 我没想到你在这里。

（五）过去进行时

1. 定义

过去进行时表示过去某个具体时刻正在进行的事情或发生的动作。

2. 结构

主语+was/ were +doing（现在分词）

3. 用法

➡ 过去进行时表示过去某段时间内持续进行的动作或者事情。常用的时间状语为 this morning、the whole morning、all day yesterday、from nine to ten last evening、when、while等。

例：We were watching TV from seven to nine last night. 昨天晚上七点到九点我们在看电视。

What was he researching all day last Sunday? 上周日他一整天都在研究什么？

My brother fell and hurt himself while he was riding his bicycle. 我哥哥骑自行车的时候从车上摔下来，受伤了。

It was raining when they left the station. 他们离开车站的时候正在下雨。

When I got to the top of the mountain, the sun was shining. 当我到达山顶的时候，阳光灿烂。

➡ 过去进行时可以表示在过去某个时间点发生的事情。时间点可以用介词短语、副词或从句来表示。

例：What was she doing at nine o'clock yesterday? 她昨天晚上九点在做什么？（介词短语表示时间点）

When I saw him he was decorating his room. 当我看见他的时候他正在装饰房间。（when从句表示时间点）

➡ 在复合句中，如果主要动作和背景动作都是延续的或同时发生的，那么主从句的动词都可用过去进行时。

例：While he was waiting for the bus，he was reading a newspaper. 他边等车边看报纸。（两个动作都是延续的）

He was cleaning his car while I was cooking. 他在洗车，我在做饭。（两个动作同时进行）

➡ 表示在过去即将发生的动作。

例：She asked him whether he was coming back for supper. 她问他是否回来吃晚饭。

➡ 表示过去的反复性或习惯性的动作，常与副词 always、constantly、continually、frequently 等连用，常常带有说话人的某种感情色彩。

例：His mother was always working like that. 他母亲总是那样工作。

➡ 通常不能用于过去进行时的动词主要有：believe、belong、care、forget、hate、have（拥有）、hear、know、like、love、mean、mind、notice、own、remember、seem、suppose、understand、want、wish 等。

（六）一般将来时

1. 定义
一般将来时表示将来某一时刻的动作或状态，或将来某一段时间内经常发生的动作或状态，或者表示计划、打算、准备做的事。

2. 结构
主语+will/ shall+动词原形

主语+am/ is/ are +going+to+动词原形

3. 用法
➡ 一般将来时表示将要发生的动作或情况。

例：I shall（will）arrive tomorrow. 我明天（会）到。（主语是第一人称时最好用 shall）

Will you be free tonight? 你今晚有空吗？

We won't（shan't）be busy this evening. 我们今晚不忙。

➔ 在一般将来时的句子中，有时有时间状语，有时没有时间状语。没有时间状语时就要从意思上判断是否指未来的动作或情况。

例：Will she come? 她（会）来吗？

➔ 在以第一人称I或we做主语的问句中，一般使用助动词shall，这时或是征求对方的意见，或是询问一个情况。

例：Where shall we meet? 我们在哪儿碰头？

Shall we have any classes tomorrow? 明天我们有课吗？

➔ be going to + 动词原形

（a）表示计划、打算、准备做的事

（b）表示即将发生或肯定要发生的事

例：We are going to put up a building here. 我们打算在这里盖一栋楼房。

How are you going to spend your holidays? 假期你准备怎样过？

I think it is going to snow. 我看要下雪了。

（七）过去完成时

1. 定义

过去完成时表示过去某一时间前就已经发生或完成了的动作，对过去的某一点造成了某种影响或是结果，用来指在另一个过去行动之前就已经完成了的事件。

2. 结构

主语+ had +动词过去分词

3. 用法

➔ 表示某一动作在过去某一时刻之前已完成。

例：By the age of 10, he had learned to play the piano for five years. 他在10岁的时候，已经学了五年钢琴。

I found your coat after you had left the house. 你离开房子之后，我发现了你的外衣。

➔ 表示由过去的某一时刻开始，一直延续到过去另一时间的动作或状态。

例：I had been at the bus stop for 20 minutes when a bus finally came. 最终当公交车来的时候，我在车站已等了20分钟。

When he had stayed here for two or three days he began to feel at home. 他在这儿住了两三天后，才觉得没有什么拘束。

4. 各种时态需要注意的几点

➡ 一个句子应该用什么时态取决于它需要表达的意思，以及它所处的语言环境。

例：He speaks English. （一般现在时，说明主语现在的情况。）

He spoke English when he was in New Zealand. （一般过去时，说明动作发生的时间。）

He is speaking English. （现在进行时，说明动作正在进行。）

He has spoken English for three years since he came to the USA. （现在完成时，这里说明动作持续的时间。）

He has been speaking English since he came to the USA. （现在完成进行时，强调动作的连续性。）

➡ 在含有时间状语从句或条件状语从句的主从复合句中，如果主句的谓语动词是一般将来时，那么从句的谓语动词就只能用一般现在时来表示将来时；如果主句的谓语动词是过去将来时，那么从句的谓语动词就只能用一般过去时表示过去将来时。

例：I will not play tennis if it rains tomorrow. （主句一般将来时，从句一般现在时）

I would not play tennis if it rained the next day. （主句过去将来时，从句一般过去时）

➡ 有些动词表示无法持续的动作，它们一般不宜用于进行时态中。

这类动词常见的有：be、believe、consist、find、forget、hate、have、hope、hear、know、like、love、notice、prefer、remember、see、seem、smell、suggest、taste、understand、want、wish、sit down、stand up等。

be动词若是用于进行时态，可表示暂时、短暂的情况或表现。

例：Tom is being a good boy today. 汤姆今天很乖。

He is being childish. 他这样做是耍孩子气。

You are not being modest. 你这样说不太谦虚。

针对上面讲到的常用时态，下面将结合考生在写作中运用到的具体句子进行讲解，使考生对时态的运用情况有一个清晰的了解。

例1.

Hi Maggie,

（1）How is Europe so far? （2）I can't wait to hear about your crazy round the world trip. （3）Which countries have you been to so far? （4）Which has been your favourite? （5）When you get a minute, send me an update. （6）I'd love to hear how it's going. （7）As for me, it's same-old-same-old. （8）At least I have a part-time job at the bookstore to keep me busy. （9）It's not much, but at least I can dream by looking at travel books. （10）How lucky you are to actually be there! （11）Anyway, I miss you and can't wait to hear from you. （12）While you're at it, send me some pictures!

Write soon!
Kitty

　　读完上面这封邮件可以发现，这是一封朋友间往来的邮件，作者询问了朋友旅行的情况，同时介绍了自己的近况。

　　邮件主体由十二个句子构成。

　　前两个句子"How is Europe so far? I can't wait to hear about your crazy round the world trip."使用的是一般现在时，以疑问句的方式对朋友的欧洲之旅进行了询问，同时表达了自己渴望听到朋友对旅行情况的描述。

　　第三个句子和第四个句子"Which countries have you been to so far? Which has been your favourite?"使用的是现在完成时，询问朋友都去了哪些国家，其中最喜欢哪个国家。现在完成时表示参观的动作已经发生，对现在造成的影响。

　　主体部分的其他句子，作者使用的是一般现在时，描述了自己的近况，其中包括对自己兼职工作的描述。作者在书店做兼职，虽然不能出去旅行，但可以看看与旅游相关的书籍。此外需要注意的是，邮件中使用的语言较亲切、口语化，因此可以判断两人之间的关系较亲近，如get a minute、same-old-same-old等词汇的使用。

　　通过上面的邮件我们可以发现询问类邮件中通常会用到一般现在时和现在完成时，用于对现在和已发生情况的说明。

例2.

Hi Kitty，

（1）I'm having a great time on my trip! （2）Yesterday I left Melbourne for Sydney and have been enjoying the changes of the scenery. （3）After a few days in Sydney, I will go to New Zealand for the last leg of my trip. （4）Australia has been so impressive，and I'm getting excited to see New Zealand's beautiful landscape. （5）I have taken a ton of pictures so far，and if you want to see them，check out my blog. （6）Next Tuesday I will fly to Auckland，and I will check in with you again when I arrive. （7）I hope you are doing well back at home in the good China.

Love and miss you，
Maggie

例2邮件是对例1的回复，在这封邮件中，作者对自己的旅行经历进行了说明，下面来看一下作者在描述的过程中都使用了哪些时态。

邮件主体由七个句子构成。

第一个句子 "I'm having a great time on my trip!" 是一个现在进行时的简单句，表示现在存在的状态。作者对自己的旅行非常满意，表达中使用了短语 "have a great time"，同时句尾使用感叹号来表达自己在旅行中所处的兴奋状态。

第二个句子 "Yesterday I left Melbourne for Sydney and have been enjoying the changes of the scenery." 是由and连接的一个并列句，前面的分句使用的是一般过去时，标志性时间状语yesterday表示动作发生在过去，所以句子的时态为一般过去时；and后面的分句使用的是现在完成进行时，表示动作从过去一直持续到现在，并将持续到将来，说明作者非常喜欢旅行途中见到的风景。

第三个句子 "After a few days in Sydney, I will go to New Zealand for the last leg of my trip." 是含有介词短语的一般将来时简单句，表示未来要进行的活动。

第四个句子 "Australia has been so impressive，and I'm getting excited to see New Zealand's beautiful landscape." 是由and连接的一个并列句，前面的分句使用的是现在完成时，说明现在的状态，and后面的分句使用的也是现在进行时，但表示将来的含义，表达作者对将要看到的美景的期待之情。

第五个句子 "I have taken a ton of pictures so far, and if you want to see them, check out my blog." 是一个复合句，里面包含 if 引导的条件状语从句，主句 I have taken a ton of pictures so far 是现在完成时，表示已经完成的动作，条件状语从句使用的是一般现在时，表示现在存在的状态。

第六个句子 "Next Tuesday I will fly to Auckland, and I will check in with you again when I arrive." 是 and 连接的一个并列句，and 前后两个分句使用的都是一般将来时，表示将要发生的动作。

第七个句子 "I hope you are doing well back at home in the good China." 是一个含有宾语从句的复合句，主句使用的是一般现在时，从句使用的是现在进行时，表示现在的状态。

例3.

Dear Alice,

（1）I stopped by your desk this morning to say hi, but I was told by your deskmate that you called in sick this morning. （2）I am sorry to hear you are feeling under the weather and hope you feel better soon. （3）With the unpredictable weather and the change of seasons, it seems everyone has been getting sick lately! （4）Make sure to keep yourself hydrated with plenty of water and vitamin C. （5）I will try to stop by your apartment later with some homemade chicken soup. （6）Some good rest should be all you need to feel like yourself in no time.

Take care and feel better!
Margarita

例3是朋友之间相互问候的邮件，发件人对收件人生病表示问候，表达了自己的关切之情，同时表示自己会去看望收件人。来看一下这封邮件中涉及的时态。

邮件主体部分包括六个句子。

第一个句子 "I stopped by your desk this morning to say hi, but I was told by your deskmate that you called in sick this morning." 是一个由 but 连接的并列句，but 前后的两个分句都为一般过去时。

第二个句子 "I am sorry to hear you are feeling under the weather and hope you feel better soon." 是一个由 and 连接的并列句，其中 and 前面的分句中还含有一个宾语从句，分句中使用的是一般现在时，对现在的状态进行说明，宾语从句中使用的是现在进行时，对朋友目前的经历进行描述；and 之后的句子省略了主语 I，使用的是一般现在时。

第三个句子 "With the unpredictable weather and the change of seasons, it seems everyone has been getting sick lately!" 中包含介词短语 with the unpredictable weather and the change of seasons，其中主句为包含表语从句的主系表结构，主句使用的是一般现在时，表语从句使用的是现在完成进行时，其中副词 lately 是典型的现在完成时态标志，表示过去一段时间以来，生病的人一直很多。

第四个句子 "Make sure to keep yourself hydrated with plenty of water and vitamin C." 是一个祈使句，使用的是一般现在时。

第五个句子 "I will try to stop by your apartment later with some homemade chicken soup." 是一个简单句，使用的是一般将来时，说明发件人将要从事的动作。

第六个句子 "Some good rest should be all you need to feel like yourself in no time." 是一个简单句，使用的是一般现在时，是对现实情况的描述。

例4.

Dear Ms. Clark,

(1) This Tuesday afternoon I have a rather urgent doctor's appointment. (2) While I had tried to arrange an appointment for after-office hours, the latest one I was able to get in is at 4:30 p.m. (3) I am respectfully requesting to be able to leave the office at 4 p.m. Tuesday, May 22nd. (4) I have already made arrangements with the department secretary to clear my Tuesday afternoon schedule. (5) If necessary, I can ask my doctor to provide work excuse documentation. (6) I appreciate your understanding.

Thank you!
(Signature)

观察例4，根据邮件内容可了解到，这是公司员工向领导发送的请假邮件。在邮件中，发件人对请假的事由和相关安排做了说明。

第一个句子 "This Tuesday afternoon I have a rather urgent doctor's appointment."

使用的是一般现在时，对现在的状态进行说明。

第二个句子"While I had tried to arrange an appointment for after-office hours, the latest one I was able to get in is at 4:30 p.m."是一个复合句，里面含有一个由while引导的让步状语从句，说明发件人曾努力想要把预约时间定在下班之后，但没有成功，这里需要注意，while引导的让步状语从句使用的是过去完成时，说明动作发生的时间在过去的某个时间点之前。逗号后面的主句为一般现在时，用于对现在状态的陈述；注意主句中包含一个定语从句，定语从句的时态为一般过去时，这里表示的是当时能安排的最晚的预约，描述的是过去的动作，所以使用一般过去时。

第三个句子"I am respectfully requesting to be able to leave the office at 4 p.m. Tuesday, May 22nd."使用的是现在进行时，发件人在这里使用现在进行时表达对未来的一种期盼，希望请假获得批准。

第四个句子"I have already made arrangements with the department secretary to clear my Tuesday afternoon. schedule."使用的是现在完成时，说明过去完成的动作对现在造成的影响。

第五个句子"If necessary, I can ask my doctor to provide work excuse documentation."使用的是一般现在时，对目前的情况进行说明。

第六个句子"I appreciate your understanding."也使用一般现在时，表达了发件人的感激之情。

（八）从句表达

英文表达中，根据语法功能的不同将从句分为：主语从句、表语从句、定语从句、同位语从句、宾语从句和状语从句六类。对于在领思写作考试中经常用到的几类从句表达，下面将详细说明：

1. 定语从句

定语从句是由关系代词或关系副词引导的从句，其作用是做定语修饰主句的某个名词性成分，相当于形容词，所以又称为形容词性从句，一般紧跟在它所修饰的先行词后面。

被定语从句修饰的那个名词叫做先行词，引导定语从句的词叫做关系词。关系词的作用是代替先行词并在定语从句中充当一定的成分。关系词分为关系代词和关系副词。关系代词有that、which、who、whom、whose、as 等，关系副词有where、when、why 等。关系词常有三个作用：

a. 连接作用，引导定语从句。

b. 代替主句中的先行词，甚至可能是主句中的一部分或者整个主句。

c. 在定语从句中充当句子成分。

➡ 关系代词who、whom、that、whose引导的定语从句

这些词代替的先行词是与人相关的名词或代词，who做主语指人，whom做宾语指人，that既可做主语又可做宾语（做宾语可以省略），可以指人也可以指物。whose用来指人或物，只用做定语。

例：（1）Is he the man who/that wants to see you? 他是那个想见你的男人吗？（who/ that在从句中做主语）

（2）He is the man whom/ that I saw yesterday. 他就是我昨天看见的那个人。（whom/ that在从句中做宾语）

（3）The man whom you spoke to just now is our English teacher. 刚才和你说话的那个男人是我们的英语老师。（whom在从句中做宾语）

（4）The man whose son is a doctor is our professor. 儿子是医生的那个男人是我们的教授。（whose在从句中做定语）

➡ 由which、that引导的从句

which、that所代替的先行词是表示事物的名词或代词，在从句中可做主语、宾语等，做宾语时可以省略。

例：（1）Prosperity which/ that had never been seen before appeared in the countryside. 农村出现了前所未有的繁荣。（which/ that在从句中做主语）

（2）The package（which/ that）you are carrying is about to come unwrapped. 你拿着的那个包裹快要散开了。（which/ that在从句中做宾语）

▶注意，关系词代表物时多用which，但在下列情况中用that而不用which：

✦先行词是anything、everything、nothing、none等不定代词时

✦先行词由every、any、all、some、no、little、few、much等修饰时，这时的that常被省略

✦先行词前有序数词或被形容词最高级修饰时

✦先行词中既有人又有物时

✦整个句子前面已有which、who、that时

✦当先行词为物并做表语时

✦先行词为one时

✦先行词同时又被the only、the very、the same修饰时

➡ 关系副词引导的定语从句

✦when指时间，在定语从句中做时间状语，也可做连接词。

例：I still remember the day when I first came to the school. 我仍然记得我第一次来学校的那一天。

✦where指地点，在定语从句中做地点状语。

例：Shanghai is the city where I was born. 上海是我出生的城市。

✦why指原因，在定语从句中做原因状语，用在reason后面。

例：Please tell me the reason why you missed the plane. 请告诉我你错过飞机的原因。

➡限制性定语从句和非限制性定语从句

定语从句有两类，即限制性定语从句和非限制性定语从句。

✦限制性定语从句

指对被修饰名词或代词的必需修饰，是被修饰名词或代词不可缺少的修饰语，如果去掉它句子意思往往会不明确甚至失去意义。

例：That's the bridge he designed. 这就是他设计的桥梁。（若把he designed去掉，句子意思则不清楚）

Madame Curie was a woman we admired. 居里夫人是我们崇拜的女性。（若把we admired去掉，句子则失去意义）

✦非限制性定语从句

非限制性定语从句和主句（句子的其他部分）关系不太紧密，对所修饰词的意思没有限制作用，把它拿掉对句子基本上没有影响，句子依然完整。它可以说是一个附加上去的成分，通常都用逗号把它和句子的其他部分分开，译成汉语时常可译成并列句。

例：Peter, who had been driving all day, suggested stopping at the next town. 彼得开了一天的车，建议在下一个城镇停一停。

I passed the letter to Helen, who was sitting beside me. 我把信传给海伦，她就坐在我旁边。

Anne, whose children are at school all day, is trying to get a job. 安妮的孩子们全天上学，她在设法找一份工作。

This is Harry, whose class you'll be taking over. 这是哈利，你将接手他的班。

My new car, which I paid several thousand pounds for, is not running well. 我的那辆新车花了我好几千英镑，开起来却不太好。

2. 宾语从句

宾语从句是名词性从句的一种。在主从复合句中充当宾语，位于及物动词、介词或复合谓语之后的从句称为宾语从句。宾语从句分为三类：动词的宾语从句，介词的宾语从句和形容词的宾语从句。

➡ 宾语从句中引导词的用法

✦ 从属连词

连接宾语从句的从属连词主要有 that、if、whether。

that 引导表示陈述的宾语从句；if 和 whether 引导表示"是否"的一般疑问句的宾语从句。

例：I felt that she had a strong will. 我感到她有坚强的意志。

  I don't know if there will be a bus any more. 我不知道是否还有公交车。

  Nobody knew whether he could pass the exam. 没人知道他是否会通过考试。

✦ 连接代词

连接代词主要有 who、whom、whose、what、whoever、whomever、whatever、whichever 等。连接代词一般表疑问，但 what、whatever 除了表疑问外，也可以表陈述。

例：Do you know who has won Red Alert game? 你知道是谁赢得了红色警报游戏吗？

  The book will show you what the best CEO should know. 这本书会告诉你最好的执行总裁该了解什么。

  Have you determined which you should buy, an Apple or Huawei cell phone? 你已经决定是买苹果还是华为手机了吗？

✦ 连接副词

连接副词主要有 when、where、why、how、whenever、wherever、however 等。

例：He didn't tell me when we should meet again. 他没有告诉我什么时候我们能再见面。

  Could you please tell me how you use the new panel? 你能告诉我你怎么用这个新的操作盘吗？

  None of us knows where these new parts can be bought. 没有人知道这些新零件能在哪里买到。

宾语从句分为三类：动词的宾语从句，介词的宾语从句和形容词的宾语从句。下面将对三种从句分别进行举例说明。

➡ 动词的宾语从句

✦ 大多数动词都可以带宾语从句，如下所示：

例：We all expect that they will win, for members of their team are stronger. 我们

都期望他们会赢，因为他们的队员更强大。

He told us that they would help us through the whole work. 他告诉我们，在整个工作中，他们都会帮忙的。

✦ 常见的能跟that的动词有：

acknowledge	add	admit	advise	agree
allege	announce	answer	assure	boast
believe	claim	command	comment	complain
confess	confirm	decide	demand	deny
determine	direct	discover	（not）doubt	dream
estimate	expect	explain	fear	feel
find	forget	guarantee	guess	hear
hint	hope	imagine	inform	insist
intend	know	learn	maintain	mean
move	order	predict	prefer	promise
propose	prove	provide	read	realize
recommend	remember	reply	report	request
require	reveal	say	see	sense
shout	show	suggest	suppose	suspect
swear	tell	think	urge	vote
wish	write			

✦ 有时可用it做先行宾语，而把从句放到主句后部去：

例：You can depend upon it, I shall be there. 你放心，我会去那里的。

I feel it a pity that I haven't been to the get-together. 我没去聚会，感觉很遗憾。

I take it they have left for home. 我猜想他们已经动身回家了。

Why don't you bring it to his attention that you're too ill to go on working? 你为什么不让他注意到你病得厉害，不能继续工作？

We all find it important that we（should）make a quick decision about this matter. 我们都认为对这件事马上做出决定很重要。

She has seen to it that all the children are well taken care of. 她已设法让所有孩子都得到了很好的照顾。

➜ 介词的宾语从句

✦ 用疑问词引导的介词宾语从句

例：We are talking about whether we admit students into our club. 我们正讨论是否让学生加入我们的俱乐部。

The new book is about how Shenzhou 6 manned spaceship was sent up into space. 这本新书是关于神舟六号载人航天飞船如何升入太空的。

✦ 用that、if引导的介词宾语从句

有时候except、but、besides三个介词后可见到由that引导的宾语从句

例：I know nothing about my new neighbor except that he used to work with a company. 对于我的新邻居我只知道他曾在一家公司上班，其他一无所知。

➡ 形容词的宾语从句

常用来引导宾语从句的形容词有：sure、certain、glad、pleased、happy、sorry、afraid、satisfied、surprised

例：I am sure I will pass the exam. 我确信我会通过考试。

I am sorry that I have troubled you so long. 很抱歉打扰你这么久。

He is glad that Li Ming went to see him when he was ill. 他很高兴在他生病的时候李明能去看望他。

➡ 宾语从句的时态用法

✦ 主句是一般现在时，从句根据实际情况可以使用任何时态。

例：She says（that）she works from Monday to Friday. 她说她从周一至周五上班。（从句是一般现在时）

She says（that）she will leave a message on his desk. 她说她要在他桌子上留个便条。（从句是一般将来时）

✦ 主句是过去时，从句须用过去时的某种形式。

例：He said（that）there were no classes yesterday afternoon. 他说昨天下午没有课。（从句是一般过去时）

He said（that）he was going to take care of the baby. 他说他会去照看这个婴儿。（从句是过去将来时）

✦ 当宾语从句表示的是一个客观真理或者事实时，即使主句是过去时，从句也用一般现在时。

例：The teacher told us（that）nothing is difficult if we put our hearts into it. 老师告诉我们世上无难事，只怕有心人。

She said（that）her father is twenty-eight years older than her. 她说她父亲比

她大二十八岁。

He said（that）light travels much faster than sound. 他说光比声音传播速度更快。

▶注意：当主句的谓语动词是think或believe，宾语从句要表达否定含义时，要把从句的否定转移到主句上；如果宾语从句有它的补语时，宾语从句用it代替，从句后置。其句型为：主语+谓语+ it +补语+宾语从句。

例：I don't think he is going to help you with your English. 我认为在学英语上他不会帮你的。

I think it necessary that we learn English grammar. 我认为我们学习英语语法是必要的。

3. 同位语从句

在复合句主句中，名词性成分之后与该名词性成分并列，补充说明该名词性成分的有关情况的名词性从句，被称为同位语从句。

➔ 同位语从句的先行词

被同位语从句所修饰的名词称为先行词。不是所有的名词都可以跟同位语从句，常可以被同位语从句修饰的名词有：belief、doubt、explanation、hope、idea、news、option、possibility、statement、thought、wish、truth、fact、question、promise、problem、reply、report、suggestion、advice、order、fear、warning、understanding、feeling、probability等。

➔ 同位语从句的引导词

引导同位语从句的词通常有连词that、whether；连接代词what、who、whom、whose、which；连接副词how、when、where等。

✦ 连词whether引导的同位语从句

例：He hasn't made the decision whether he will go there. 他还没有做出决定是否去那里。

I have small doubt whether he is suitable for the job. 他是否适合这份工作我有点怀疑。

✦ 连词that引导的同位语从句

例：We came to the decision that we must act at once. 我们做出决定：我们必须立即行动。

He made a proposal that the meeting be postponed. 他提议会议延期。

There was little hope that he would survive. 他幸存的希望渺茫。

◆连接代词what、who、whom、whose、which引导的同位语从句

例：I have no idea what he is doing now. 我不知道他现在在干什么。

The question who should replace her requires consideration. 谁该代替她，这个问题需要考虑。

I have no idea what size of shoes she wears. 我不知道她穿几号的鞋。

◆连接副词how、when、where、why引导的同位语从句

例：She raised the question where we could get the fund. 她提出这个问题：我们到哪儿去搞这笔资金。

I have no idea when she will be back. 我不知道她什么时候回来。

The teacher had no idea why Jack was absent. 老师不知道杰克为什么缺勤。

4. 状语从句

按照功能来划分，状语从句主要分为九类，分别为：时间状语从句、条件状语从句、目的状语从句、结果状语从句、原因状语从句、让步状语从句、方式状语从句、地点状语从句和比较状语从句。下面将对这几种从句中较常用的几类引导词和用法分别进行说明。

➡（1）时间状语从句

用表示时间的连词连接一个句子做状语，这样的主从复合句就是时间状语从句。连接时间状语从句的连接词有：when、while、as、before、after、until、till、since、as soon as、by the time、whenever等。下面将对这些连接词的具体用法进行简要说明：

◆when的用法

when的意思是"当……时"，表示主句动作发生的特定时间，when引导的从句的谓语动词可以是延续性的，也可以是瞬时性的。

▶when意为"当……时""在……之后"，引导时间状语从句，表示主句的动作和从句的动作同时或先后发生。

例：When we cross the street, we must be careful. 我们过马路时，一定要小心。

When he comes I'll tell him about it. 他来时我将把这事告诉他。

▶when引导的时间状语从句中的动词可以是延续性动词，也可以是终止性动词。

例：He was writing his homework when I went into the classroom. 当我走进教室的时候，他正在写作业。

◆while的用法

while引导时间状语从句时常译为"与……同时，在……期间"，强调主句动作和从句动作是同时发生的。while引导的从句中的动词常用延续性动词或表示状态的动词。

例：While my sister was cooking, I was sweeping the floor. 我姐姐在做饭时，我在扫地。（while表示两个动作同时发生）

While doing so, we decided to sell the boat. 在这样做时，我们决定把船卖掉。

▶注意：在 when 和 while引导的从句中，当主句和从句的主语一致，并且从句中有be动词时，可以省略主语和be动词（构成when/ while+-ing结构）。

例：When（she is）in trouble, she always asks for the teacher's help. 她遇到困难时总是向老师求助。

While（I am）travelling, I like to buy some souvenirs. 旅游时我喜欢买纪念品。

✦as的用法

as引导时间状语从句时可以表达"正当……，一边……一边……；随着……"等意思，as在引导时间状语从句时，有以下三种用法：

▶表示某事一发生，另一件事随即发生。

例：As the sun rose, the fog disappeared. 太阳一出来，雾就消散了。

▶表示某事发生的过程中另一件事也在发生。

例：I heard their murmurs as I crossed the hall. 我走过大厅的时候听到他们在嘀咕什么。

▶表示两个动作同时发生。

例：He smiled as he passed. 他路过的时候笑了一下。（两个都是短暂动作）

He saw that she was smiling as she read. 他看到她一边看书一边笑。（两个都是延续性动作）

✦before/ after的用法

▶before引导的时间状语从句通常表示主句的动作发生在从句的动作之前，反之则用after。

before的意思是"在……之前"、表示主句动作发生在从句动作之前。

例：Close the windows before you leave the classroom, please. 在你离开教室前，请关上窗。

It wasn't long before he told us about it. 不久他就把这事告诉我们了。

▶after的意思是"在……之后"，表示主句的动作发生在从句的动作之后。

例：I went to school after I finished my breakfast. 我吃完早饭后去上学。

She showed me many beautiful photos after I got to her home. 我到她家以后，

她让我看了好多漂亮的照片。

✦until/ till 的用法

▶until/ till 引导时间状语从句，主句的谓语动词是延续性动词时，主句用肯定形式表示这一动作或状态一直延续到 until/ till 所表示的时间为止。until 和 till 都表示"直到"，常可换用，但 till 不用于句首，也不可用于强调句。

例：We danced and danced until they all joined in us. 我们不停地跳舞，直到他们都参加进来。

▶主句谓语动词是非延续性动词时，用否定形式表示主句的谓语所表示的动作直到until 所表示的时间才发生。

构成句式 not...until...，有时不用 not，而用其他如 never、nothing 等表示否定的词。

例：He didn't go to bed until he had finished his homework. 他直到做完作业才上床睡觉。

✦since 的用法

since 引导的时间状语从句，表示"自……以来"，主句用一般现在时或现在完成时，从句用一般过去时或现在完成时。

例：They have been friends since they were at primary school. 他们从小学起就一直是好朋友。

He has never been to see me since I have been ill. 我生病以来他从未来看过我。

▶注意：since 引导的从句的谓语动词可以是延续性动词，也可以是瞬时动词。

✦as soon as 的用法

as soon as 引导的从句表示从句的动作一发生，主句的动作随即发生，常译为"一……就……"，该从句经常用一般现在时表示将来。

例：We began to work as soon as we got there. 我们一到那里就开始工作。

As soon as he arrives, I'll tell him. 他一到，我就告诉他。

✦by the time 的用法

这个词组常用来指到某一时间点为止，主句常用完成时态。

例：By the time you arrived, the film had already ended. 你到的时候，电影已经结束了。

✦whenever 的用法

whenever 引导时间状语从句表示"每当，一……就……"，与 when 的用法相似，但语气更强。

例：The roof leaks whenever it rains. 这屋顶一下雨就漏。

　　You can borrow my car whenever you want. 你随时可以借我的车。

→（2）条件状语从句

在句子中做条件状语的从句称为条件状语从句。条件状语从句可置于句首，也可以置于句尾，有时还可置于主语和谓语之间。条件状语从句的常用引导词为：if、unless、as/ so long as、once、in case、on condition that、supposing（that）、providing（that）、provided（that）、given（that）等。下面的内容将对主要引导词的使用情况及条件状语从句的时态进行举例说明。

✦if的用法

▶引导条件状语从句最常用的连词是if，由if引导的条件状语从句表示在某种条件下某事很可能发生。

例：If it doesn't rain tomorrow, we'll go to the Great Wall. 如果明天不下雨，我们就去长城。

　　If you fail in the exam, you will let him down. 如果你考试不及格，你会让他失望的。

▶另外，if从句还表示不可实现的条件或根本不可能存在的条件，也就是一种虚拟的条件或假设，从句多用一般过去时或过去完成时。条件状语从句分为真实条件状语从句和非真实条件状语从句。

如：If I were you, I would invite him to the party. 如果我是你，我会邀请他参加聚会。

　　The flower would not have died if I had watered them before I left home. 如果我在离开家之前浇了水，这些花就不会死了。

✦unless的用法

unless意为"除非，若不，除非在……的时候"。

例：Courage is doing what you're afraid to do. There can be no courage unless you are scared. 勇气就是去做你所畏惧的事情。只有当你胆怯时才有勇气可言。

　　Victory won't come to us unless we go to it. 胜利不会走向我们，我们必须自己走向胜利。

　　Unless it rains, the game will be played. 除非下雨，否则比赛将照常进行。

▶注意：unless的意思相当于if...not...。上面的最后两个例子可变为：

Victory won't come to us if we don't go to it.

If it doesn't rain, the game will be played.

✦on condition（that）...的用法

on condition（that）...引导的条件状语从句是主句事件发生的前提条件或唯一条件，意为"在……条件下"。

例：I can tell you the truth on condition that you promise to keep it a secret. 我可以告诉你真相，条件是你答应保守秘密。

Ron lent me the money on condition that I pay it back next month. 罗恩把钱借给我，条件是下月归还。

✦supposing/ provided/ providing/ given（that）的用法

supposing/ providing/ provided（that）可以做连词，意为"如果"，引导的条件从句表示一种假设条件。这几个词意义相近。

例：Supposing（that）something should go wrong, what would you do then? 假如出了问题，你会怎么办？

I don't mind Jerry's coming with us, provided/ providing（that）he pays for his own meal. 只要杰瑞自付餐费，我不介意他和我们一起去。

Providing/ Supposing/ Given/ Provided（that）you promise not to tell anyone else, I'll explain the secret. 只要你保证不告诉任何人，我就把这个秘密告诉你。

➜ 条件状语从句的时态

条件状语从句的时态由主句决定。主句是一般将来时态、祈使句或含有情态动词的一般现在时，从句要用现在时态；主句如果是过去的某种时态，则从句要用过去的某种时态。

➜ （3）目的状语从句

在句中做目的状语的从句称为目的状语从句。目的状语从句可置于句首、句中或句尾。常用来引导目的状语从句的关联词有：so、so that、in order that、for fear that、in case（that）、for the purpose that、lest等。下面将对这些连接词的具体用法进行简要说明：

✦in order that、so that引导的目的状语从句

in order that常用于正式文体，可置于句首，也可置于句尾；so that往往只置于句尾，在个别情况下也可置于句首，so that短语中有时可省略that。

例：We shall let you know the details soon so that/ in order that you can/ may make your arrangements. 不久我们将会让你知道详情，以便你们能够做出安排。

My father has bought me a bicycle so that/ in order that I can get to school quickly. 我爸给我买了辆自行车，以便我能快速赶到学校。

✦for fear（that）、in case、lest引导的目的状语从句

for fear（that）表示目的时，意为"唯恐，以防"；in case意为"以免，以防有某种情况发生"；lest意为"以防"。这三个短语或词都相当于in order that...not..., so that...not...。

例：Shut the window lest/ in case it should rain. 关上窗，以防下雨。

The victims all seemed afraid to say the facts, for fear it might start trouble. 受害人似乎都不敢说出真相，怕引起麻烦。

She pulled away from the window lest anyone（should）see her. 她从窗口躲开了，免得有人见到她。

I shall stay in the hotel all day in case there is news of Henry. 我将一整天待在旅馆里，以防有亨利的消息。

➜（4）结果状语从句

在句子中做结果状语的从句称为结果状语从句。结果状语从句一般置于句尾。常用来引导结果状语从句的引导词或短语有：so、so that、so...that...、such that、such...that...、that等。下面将对这些连接词的具体用法进行简要说明：

✦so that与so...that...引导的结果状语从句

so that/ so...that...引导结果状语从句，意为"如此……以至于"，在口语中，that常可省略。

例：We moved to the country so that we were away from the noisy and dull city. 我们搬到了乡下，所以我们远离了喧嚣、单调的城市。

She is ill so that she can't attend the meeting this afternoon. 她病了，不能参加今天下午的会议了。

▶so...that...引导的结果状语从句可以构成如下结构：

so+形容词/ 副词+that

so+形容词+a/ an+单数名词+that

so+many/ few （+可数名词复数）+that

so+much/ little+（不可数名词）+that

例：The wind was so strong that he could hardly move forward. 风刮得如此猛烈，以致他几乎寸步难行。

It was so hot a day that they wanted to go swimming. 天那么热，他们想去

游泳。

There are so many picture-story books that the boy won't leave. 有那么多连环画书，男孩都不想离开了。

He gave me so little time that it was impossible for me to finish the work on time. 他给我的时间如此少，要我按时完成这份工作是不可能的。

▶such（...）that...引导的结果状语从句可构成如下结构：

such + a/ an+形容词+单数名词+that

such+形容词+可数名词复数+that

such+形容词+不可数名词+that

例：Kathy is such a young girl that she can't go to school. 凯西年龄太小，还不能去上学。

They are such fine teachers that we all hold them in great respect. 他们是非常好的老师，我们都对他们极为尊敬。

It is such nice weather that I would like to go to the beach. 天气如此之好，我想去海滩。

▶注意：为了强调形容词或副词，so/ such...that...引导的结果状语从句可把so/ such置于句首，主句用倒装语序。

例：So carelessly did he drive that he nearly got killed. 他开车如此粗心，差点丧命。

Such good news did we get that everyone was excited. 我们得到这么好的消息，以致每个人都很兴奋。

→ （5）原因状语从句

原因状语从句指在句中用来说明主句原因的从句。引导原因状语从句的常用词可分为两类：单词和短语。单词主要有because、since、as等；短语主要有now that、seeing that、for the reason that、in that、considering（that）等，下面将对这些连接词的具体用法进行简要说明：

✦because引导的原因状语从句

because表因果关系的语气最强，用来回答以why提问的问句，所引出的原因往往是听话人所不知道或最感兴趣的。because引导的原因状语从句往往比主句显得更重要。

例：Big goals are necessary because you must see it big before you can make it big. 远大的目标是必要的，因为你在实现远大的目标前，必须视其为远大的目标。

He is absent today because he is ill. 因为他生病了，所以今天没来。

✦since引导的原因状语从句

表示人们已知的事实，不需强调原因，故常译为"既然……"，通常放在句首。since引导的从句是次要的，重点强调主句的内容。

例：Since you are so sure of it, he'll believe you. 既然你对此这么有把握，他会相信你的。

Since tomorrow is Jim's birthday, let's give him a party. 既然明天是吉姆的生日，那我们举行一个聚会吧。

✦as引导的原因状语从句

as与since用法差不多，所引出的理由在说话人看来已经很明显，或已为听话人所熟悉，也不须用because加以强调。as引导的从句与主句有同等的地位。

例：We have to delay our journey, as the weather is so bad. 天气太恶劣了，我们不得不推迟行程。

As rain has fallen, the air is cooler. 因为下过雨，空气更清凉了。

✦其他引导词连接的原因状语从句

now that、seeing that、for the reason that、in that、considering（that）等也可引导原因状语从句。

例：Now that they've got to know each other a little better, they get along just fine. 由于彼此间有了进一步的了解，他们相处得不错。

Seeing that he is inexperienced, he is not fit for the work. 既然他没有经验，他就不适合这项工作。

I often go to the cinema for the simple reason that I love seeing films. 我经常去看电影，原因很简单，那就是因为我喜欢看电影。

I like the city, but I prefer the country in that there is fresher air. 我喜欢城市，但我更喜欢乡村，因为那里有更清新的空气。

Considering（that）he hasn't fully recovered yet, it will not be proper to assign him such a hard job. 考虑到他身体还没有完全恢复，不适合指派他干这么难的工作。

➔（6）让步状语从句

在句中表示让步关系的从句称为让步状语从句，一般翻译为"尽管……"或"即使……"，相当于日常生活中的"退一步说……"的感觉。让步状语从句既可置于主句之前，也可置于主句之后。引导让步状语从句的连词有although、though、even if、even though、as、whether... or...、whether（...）or not、while、whatever、no matter what/ how/ why等。下面将对这些连接词的具体用法进行简要说明：

✦though/ although引导的让步状语从句

although和though意义一样，意为"虽然，即使"，都表示让步，一般情况下可互换使用。although语气较重，大多置于句首。though/ although引导让步状语从句时，主句若用yet或still引出，更加强调对比性，但不可出现but。有时也用于倒装句型。as though、even though一般不可用although代替。同时although不可当副词用，而though可以。

例：They are generous though they are poor. 虽然他们很穷，但他们很慷慨。

Although she was tired, she stayed up to watch the late night film on television. 虽然她很累，她还是熬夜看电视上的午夜电影。

Though he had very little money, he always managed to dress smartly. 虽说他没几个钱，却总是设法穿得时髦潇洒。

✦even though/ even if引导的让步状语从句

even though和even if这两个短语表示语气更强的让步，常常意为"再退一步说"。even though更侧重对"既成事实"的让步，even if更侧重对"假设"的让步。

例：Even though not large, the room was light and airy. 房间虽然不大，采光和通风却很好。

Even if he is poor, she loves him. （=He may be poor, yet she loves him.）即使他很穷，但她还是爱他。

Even though he is poor, she loves him. 尽管他很穷，但她还是爱他。（=He is poor, yet she loves him.）

✦as引导的让步状语从句

as表示"让步"时常用倒装。倒装时若有带冠词的名词，冠词需要省去。as的这种用法与though倒装时的用法一致，although则不可这样使用。

例：Urgent as/ though the message is, it is impossible to send it there in time.

（=Though the message is urgent, it is impossible to send it there in time.）

消息很紧急，但不可能及时送到。

Child as/ though he was, he faced the dangerous situation calmly.

（=Though he was a child, he faced the dangerous situation calmly.）

尽管还是个孩子，但他能冷静地面对危险情况。

Much as he loves his daughter, he is strict with her.

他很爱女儿，但对她管教很严。

Object as you may, I'll go.

（=Though/ Although you may object, I'll go.）

纵使你反对，我也要去。

✦whether...or.../　whether（...）or not引导的让步状语从句

whether...or.../　whether（...）or not表示"不论是否……""不管是……还是……"之意。由其引导的让步状语从句主要用于表达正反两个方面的可能性都不影响主句的意向或结果。

例：Whether you believe it or not, it's true. 无论你是否相信，这都是真的。

　　I'll marry him whether he is poor or rich. 不管他是穷还是富，我都要和他结婚。

✦while引导的让步状语从句

while也可以引导让步状语从句，表示"尽管……"，比though/ although语气弱。while引导的让步状语从句一般位于句首。

例：While they are my neighbors, I don't know them well. 虽然他们是我的邻居，我对他们却不太了解。

　　While I understand what you say, I can't agree with you. 虽然我理解你的意思，但我还是不同意你的观点。

✦wh-ever类词引导的让步状语从句

在英语中，wh-ever类词可做主句的疑问词，也可引导名词性从句，还可引导让步状语从句。这类词在引导让步状语从句时常可换成no matter+相应的wh-词，在引导名词性从句时只能用wh-ever。

例：Whatever you say, I won't believe you.

（=No matter what you say, I won't believe you.）

不论你说什么，我都不会相信你。

Whenever I'm unhappy, it is my friend who cheers me up.

（=No matter when I'm unhappy, it is my friend who cheers me up.）

不管我什么时候不高兴，都是我的朋友使我振作起来。

I'll wait for you however late it is.

（=I'll wait for you no matter how late it is.）

不管多晚我都会等着你。

▶注意："no matter+疑问词"结构只能引导让步状语从句，而wh-ever类词还可以引导名词性从句。

例：Whatever（=No matter what）happened, he would not mind.

（whatever引导让步状语从句）无论发生什么，他都不会介意。

I'll take whoever（≠no matter who）wants to go.

（whoever引导宾语从句）谁想去我就带谁去。

→（7）方式状语从句

方式状语从句多用来谈论某人的行为或者做某事的方式。常用连接词有as、（just）as...so...、as if、as though、the way等。下面将对这些连接词的具体用法进行简要说明：

✦as、（just）as...so...引导的方式状语从句

as、（just）as...so...等引导的方式状语从句通常位于主句后。（just）as...so...结构位于句首时，as从句带有比喻含义，意为"正如……，就像……"，多用于正式文体。

例：You ought to do as I tell you. 你应当照我说的做。

When in Rome, do as the Romans do.（谚）入乡随俗。

As water is to fish, so air is to man. 人类离不开空气，犹如鱼儿离不开水。

✦as if/ as though引导的方式状语从句

两者的意义和用法相同，引出的状语从句多用虚拟语气，表示与事实相反；有时也用陈述语气，表示所说情况是事实或实现的可能性较大。常译为"仿佛……似的，好像……似的"。

例：I remember the whole thing as if/ as though it happened yesterday. 整件事情我都记得，就仿佛是昨天发生的一样。（与事实相反，谓语用虚拟语气）

It looks as if the weather may pick up very soon. 看来天气很快就会好起来。（实现的可能性较大，谓语用陈述语气）

→（8）地点状语从句

地点状语从句是表示地点、方位的状语从句，这类从句通常由where、wherever、everywhere引导。下面将对这些连接词的具体用法进行简要说明：

✦where引导地点状语从句

where是最为常用的引导地点状语从句的从属连词。

例：I'll drive you where you're going. 你到哪儿我都可以开车送你去。

We must camp where we can get water. 我们必须在能找到水的地方露营。

✦wherever引导地点状语从句

wherever引导地点状语从句表示"无论在哪里"的意思。

例：Wherever he goes, there's always a spy hanging about. 不管他到哪里，总有一个密探跟着。

Wherever he is, he'll be thinking of you. 不管他在哪里，他总会想着你。

✦everywhere引导地点状语从句

everywhere作为连词表示"在每个地方，无论在哪里"。

例：Everywhere they appeared there were ovations. 他们所到之处都有人欢呼。

You can find honest men everywhere you go. 你无论到哪里，都能找到诚实的人。

➔（9）比较状语从句

比较状语从句常用于含有形容词和副词的原级、比较级及最高级的句子中，是起副词作用的句子。比较状语从句一般位于句尾。比较状语从句常用as...as、not as/ so...as...、than等连接词引导。"the+比较级……，the+比较级……"结构也可引导比较状语从句。下面将对比较状语从句的用法分别进行说明。

✦同级比较

同级比较常见于如下结构中

▶ as/ so + 原级 + as 和……一样，（其中as/ so是副词，意思是"同样地"，后一个as是连词）

例：My hometown is as/ so beautiful as Beihai（is）. 我的家乡和北海一样美丽。

▶no +比较级+ than 最多和……一样，只不过

例：The woman was no older than Kate. 那个女人不比凯特大。

▶not more than，不多于

例：I have not more than two dollars left in my pocket. 我口袋里顶多还有两美元。

▶no less than 不亚于……，至少和……一样

例：He has got no less presents than I did last time. 他收到的礼品不亚于我上次收到的。

✦优级比较

▶A+比较级 + than+B，A比B更……

如：Our class is bigger than yours. 我们班的规模比你们的大。

▶the 比较级 + the 比较级，越……就越……

例：The more we can do for you, the happier we will be. 为你们做得越多，我们就越感到高兴。

✦差级比较

▶A+less + 原级 + than+B，A不及B

例：This kind of food is less expensive than that one. 这种食品不如那一种贵。

▶not so +原级+ as, 不如, 不及……

例: The film today is not so interesting as the one of yesterday. 今天的电影不如昨天的那场有意思。

针对上面讲到的各类从句表达, 下面将结合考生在写作中实际使用到的各类从句进行讲解, 使考生对从句的运用情况有一个清晰的了解。

例1.

Dear Sir or Madam,

（1）I am writing to apply for the Travel Competition that appeared on the advertisement of the Local English Language newspaper last week.（2）I would like to have the opportunity to participate in the travel competition as a member of your team.

（3）I am very interested in going on the trip because I am young, healthy and I like doing adventure sports such as climbing, skiing, paragliding, canoeing...（4）Moreover, I like sharing this kind of experiences with other people because I enjoy doing group tasks.

（5）In this moment, I am in good conditions physically and psychologically because I have been living in the Amazon Jungle under hard conditions for two months as a member of *Supervivientes* in a T.V. programme of Channel 5 in Spain.（6）We had to survive without food and water and learnt to fish and hunt.（7）It was a fantastic experience as we did great friends.

（8）I'm very glad if I could participate in a Round World trip as you mentioned.

（9）I look forward to receiving your reply as soon as possible.

Yours faithfully,

（Signature）

观察上面的学生习作可发现, 这是发件人给旅游比赛的组织者发送的一封申请邮件, 目的是申请参加当地英文报纸广告上刊登的旅游比赛活动。在这封邮件中, 作者对自己的目的及申请原因进行了详细说明。在对自身情况进行说明的过程中, 作者使用了各种不同的从句表达, 使句子更加多样化。下面将对邮件中出现的从句进行详细说明。

第一个句子 "I am writing to apply for the Travel Competition that appeared on the advertisement of the Local English Language newspaper last week." 是包含定语从句的复合句，其中that引导定语从句，对前面出现的名词Travel Competition进行解释说明。

第三个句子 "I am very interested in going on the trip because I am young, healthy and I like doing adventure sports such as climbing, skiing, paragliding, canoeing..." 是and连接的并列句，同时and前面的分句中包含一个由because引导的原因状语从句，该从句说明了作者对旅行感兴趣的原因；and后面为一个简单句。

第四个句子 "Moreover, I like sharing this kind of experiences with other people because I enjoy doing group tasks." 是包含原因状语从句的复合句，because引导的原因状语从句对作者喜欢这种经历的原因进行了说明。

第五个句子 "In this moment, I am in good conditions physically and psychologically because I have been living in the Amazon Jungle under, hard conditions for two months as a member of *Supervivientes* in a T.V. programme of Channel 5 in Spain." 是包含原因状语从句的复合句，分号后面的内容是对前面原因的解释说明。

第七个句子 "It was a fantastic experience as we did great friends." 是包含原因状语从句的复合句，as引导的原因状语从句对前面的句子进行解释说明。

第八个句子 "I'm very glad if I could participate in a Round World trip as you mentioned." 是包含条件状语从句的复合句，if对条件进行了说明。

例2.

Hi,

（1）I'm glad you asked for my help!

（2）My cousin had the same problem. （3）Home or university? （4）That is the question. （5）The answer depends on many things, mostly your plans for the future. （6）Let me tell you what happened to Jake (this is my cousin's name). （7）He had one hobby, maths. （8）He always knew that his job will be connected with it. （9）At the age of 15, Jake didn't want to learn anything else! （10）One day he had so important an exam that it was organized only in the capital of Poland. （11）Unfortunately, Jake was late. （12）Before he went to sleep, he had forgotten to ask his mother to wake him up. （13）The train had left before he got to the station. （14）Then he called his teacher and asked them for a second chance. （15）They agreed! （16）When he wrote the test, everybody was so impressed by his skills that he got an offer— "be the student of our university. We want you". （17）Then he had to choose. （18）Staying with family or going abroad? （19）He preferred home, and trust me, it was a huge mistake. （20）And that's what you should do— follow your dreams.

See you soon.
Steve

上面一篇学生习作是朋友间的信函往来，作者在信函中对自己表弟的情况进行了说明，希望能给收件人提供帮助。整篇邮件内容较口语化，句子较多。下面来看一下作者在表达的过程中都使用了哪些从句。

第一个句子 "I'm glad you asked for my help!" 是含有宾语从句的复合句，其中宾语从句 "you asked for my help!" 省略了引导词that。

第六个句子 "Let me tell you what happened to Jake." 是含有宾语从句的复合句，"what happened to Jake" 是what引导的宾语从句，做tell的直接宾语。

第八个句子 "He always knew that his job will be connected with it." 是含有宾

语从句的复合句，"that his job will be connected with it"是that引导的宾语从句，做knew的宾语。

第十个句子 "One day he had so important an exam that it was organized only in the capital of Poland." 是含有结果状语从句的复合句，在这个句子中，so+形容词+an+可数名词单数+that引导结果状语从句，对考试的重要性进行了说明。

第十三个句子 "The train had left before he got to the station." 是含有时间状语从句的复合句，在这个句子中，before引导时间状语从句，对时间的先后关系进行了说明。

第十六个句子 "When he wrote the test, everybody was so impressed by his skills that he got an offer— "be the student of our university. We want you." 是含有时间状语从句和结果状语从句的复合句，其中when引导时间状语，对句子中体现的时间关系进行了说明；同时 "that he got an offer— "be the student of our university..." 是so...that引导的结果状语从句。

第二十个句子 "And that's what you should do—follow your dreams." 是含有表语从句的复合句，"what you should do"在句子中做表语，其中破折号后面的内容是对表语的解释说明，即你应该做的就是追随你的梦想。

例3.

（1）Is it a good or bad thing to have products that last a long time? （2）Sometimes it makes us doubt about products with long life like, batteries, tvs, computers, clothes, accessories, and ect.

（3）Fashion, for example, is always changing and it is difficult to follow it. （4）Changing technology is a good idea, because the usefulness of equipment lies in its service life. （5）And when it is over the device does not work properly. （6）For bowls, mugs and so on, sometimes it is good to keep them, especially if you had taken it for a special occasion.

（7）I think we need to have a common sense to keep things, otherwise we become hoarders and it is really bad to us and for the community we live in.

（8）Furthermore, if you want to keep many products for long time, you need a space to keep them.

（9）In conclusion, whether it is good or bad to have long-lasting products depends on the people who own them. （10）In addition, people need to be conscious about our planet, because most of the long-lasting products are dangerous for the soil and the air. （11）We need to know where to leave these products when they do not work anymore.

观察上面的习作可发现，这是一篇小短文。作者在短文中陈述了自己对产品使用寿命长短的观点，并说明了其存在的利弊。短文由多个段落构成，下面来看看短文中使用到的从句。

第一个句子"Is it a good or bad thing to have products that last a long time?"是包含定语从句的复合句，that引导定语从句修饰前面的名词products。

第三个句子"Fashion, for example, is always changing and it is difficult to follow it."是由and连接的一个并列句，包含两个简单句。

第四个句子"Changing technology is a good idea, because the usefulness of equipment lies in its service life." 是包含原因状语从句的复合句，because 引导的原因状语从句对前面一句话进行了解释说明。

第五个句子 "And when it is over the device does not work properly." 是包含时间状语从句的复合句，when 引导时间状语从句。

第六个句子 "For bowls, mugs and so on, sometimes it is good to keep them, especially if you had taken it for a special occasion." 是包含条件状语从句的复合句，if 引导的条件状语从句对实现主句的条件进行了说明。

第七个句子 "I think we need to have a common sense to keep things, otherwise we become hoarders and it is really bad to us and for the community we live in." 是由 and 连接的一个并列复合句，里面包含三个简单句。

第八个句子 "Furthermore, if you want to keep many products for long time you need a space to keep them." 是包含条件状语从句的复合句，if 引导的条件状语从句对前提条件进行了说明。

第九个句子 "In conclusion, whether it is good or bad to have long-lasting products depends on the people who own them." 是包含主语从句和定语从句的复合句，其中 "whether it is good or bad to have long-lasting products" 是 whether 引导的主语从句，在句子中做主语；"who own them" 是 who 引导的定语从句，修饰前面的名词 people。

第十个句子 "In addition, people need to be conscious about our planet, because most of the long-lasting products are dangerous for the soil and the air." 是包含原因状语从句的复合句，because 引导的原因状语从句是对前一句话的解释说明。

第十一个句子 "We need to know where to leave these products, when they do not work anymore." 是包含一个宾语从句和一个时间状语从句的复合句，其中 "where to leave these products" 是 where 引导的宾语从句；"when they do not work anymore." 是 when 引导的时间状语从句。

例4.

Young people living in cities

（1）Nowadays many young people prefer to live in the big cities. （2）There are many factors that have influence on their decisions, but the most common ones are work and education.

（3）It is the job that really matters to all of us and especially to the young generation. （4）They all want a high salary, which will provide them with a good and stable life. （5）But as we know, a wider range of jobs can be found in the big cities and that is why young people choose to live there.

（6）Another reason, which is really important for students, is the education. （7）Most of the good universities are located in the cities and the young people have no choice, because the majority realize that if you want to succeed in the life, you need to have an excellent education.

（8）Also the educational system is better in towns than in villages. （9）A bigger variety of programmes is available and you can have a chance to get an internship, which will be really helpful in the future when you try to find a good job.

（10）Of course, there are more reasons, like nightlife, which will always attract the young people to choose a big city than a small one. （11）However, work and education will be the most important.

  上面的学生习作属于小短文，作者在短文中通过五个段落对年轻人在城市里生活的原因进行了说明，作者在表述的过程中使用了多种从句，下面将对使用到的从句进行详细说明。

  第二个句子 "There are many factors that have influence on their decisions, but the most common ones are work and education." 是but连接的一个并列句，其中but前

面的句子"There are many factors that have influence on their decisions"中包含一个that引导的定语从句，修饰前面的名词factors。

第四个句子"They all want a high salary, which will provide them with a good and stable life."是包含定语从句的复合句，which引导的定语从句修饰前面的名词salary。

第五个句子"But as we know, a wider range of jobs can be found in the big cities and that is why young people choose to live there."是and连接的并列句；同时and后面的句子"why young people choose to live there"是why引导的表语从句。

第六个句子"Another reason, which is really important for students, is the education."是包含定语从句的复合句，which引导的定语从句修饰前面的名词reason。

第七个句子"Most of the good universities are located in the cities and the young people have no choice, because the majority realize that if you want to succeed in the life, you need to have an excellent education."结构较复杂。because前面的部分"Most of the good universities are located in the cities and the young people have no choice"是由and连接的一个并列句，两个分句均为简单句；because后面的部分是because引导的原因状语从句，对前面的句子"年轻人别无选择"进行解释说明；在because引导的原因状语从句中，that引导宾语从句，做realize的宾语；同时that从句中还包含一个if引导的条件状语从句。

第九个句子"A bigger variety of programmes is available and you can have a chance to get an internship, which will be really helpful in the future when you try to find a good job."是由and连接的一个并列句，同时包含一个which引导的定语从句，修饰前面的名词internship；在定语从句中还包含一个由when引导的时间状语从句。

第十个句子"Of course, there are more reasons, like nightlife, which will always attract the young people to choose a big city than a small one."是包含定语从句的复合句，which引导的定语从句修饰前面的"more reasons like nightlife"。

例5.

Dear Jessie,

（1）I think it would be a good idea for you to have a part-time job. （2）When I was doing my business course, I did spend a lot of time studying, but I had a part-time job anyway. （3）Sometimes I was very busy with both studying and the job, but if you just plan the schoolwork and your job well, it won't be a problem.

（4）I would definitely recommend taking a part-time job because you will probably need the money. （5）I took a part-time job because I could not pay for the course without it.

（6）So if you are planning to search for a job, look for something where you can plan whenever you want to work, so you don't have to work when it's a bad time for you. （7）It would be very nice if you can cancel on your work, and they don't depend on you very much. （8）I took a job like that at the local supermarket. （9）When I really could not work, I always could cancel pretty easily. （10）But you can't do that too often, of course, because your boss might not like it. （11）I really liked that job.

（12）Maybe you can work at a supermarket too, or maybe another store. （13）I also knew someone who worked at a place where they sold ice cream, milkshake and frozen yoghurt. （14）She loved working there.

（15）Good luck with finding a job and with your business course!
（Signature）

　　上面的学生习作是一封电子邮件，作者在邮件中就是否应该找兼职工作一事提供了自己的想法。邮件主体部分包括四个段落，在表达的过程中作者使用了各种从句，从句的使用使句式表达更加灵活。下面将对使用到的从句进行详细说明。

　　第二个句子"When I was doing my business course, I did spend a lot of time studying, but I had a part-time job anyway." 是含有时间状语从句的复合句，其中 when 引导时间状语从句，对主句中动作发生的时间进行了说明；同时需要注意，主句是由 but 连接的并列句，并列句的两个分句均为简单句。

第四个句子 "I would definitely recommend taking a part-time job because you will probably need the money." 是含有原因状语从句的复合句，because 引导的原因状语从句对作者建议从事兼职工作的原因进行了说明。

第五个句子 "I took a part-time job because I could not pay for the course without it." 是含有原因状语从句的复合句，because 引导的原因状语从句中作者对自己从事兼职工作的原因进行了说明。

第六个句子 "So if you are planning to search for a job, look for something where you can plan whenever you want to work, so you don't have to work when it's a bad time for you." 的结构较复杂。"if you are planning to search for a job," 是 if 引导的条件状语从句；"look for something where you can plan whenever you want to work," 中包含 where 引导的定语从句，对 something 进行修饰，同时 whenever 又引导了一个时间状语从句；"so you don't have to work when it's a bad time for you"，其中 when 引导了时间状语从句。

第七个句子 "It would be very nice if you can cancel on your work, and they don't depend on you very much." 是包含条件状语从句的复合句，其中 if 引导条件状语从句，同时 if 引导的条件状语从句还是一个由 and 连接的并列句。

第九个句子 "When I really could not work, I always could cancel pretty easily." 是含有时间状语从句的复合句，其中 when 引导的时间状语从句对时间情况进行了说明。

第十个句子 "But you can't do that too often, of course, because your boss might not like it." 是含有原因状语从句的复合句，because 对前面情况的原因进行了说明。

第十三个句子 "I also knew someone who worked at a place where they sold ice cream, milkshake and frozen yoghurt." 是含有定语从句的复合句，who 引导的定语从句对前面的 someone 进行修饰；同时在定语从句中还包含一个 where 引导的定语从句，对前面的 place 进行修饰。

Day 2　提分篇——电子邮件格式及常用表达

一、电子邮件格式和结构

From:	Michael Bull
To:	Rock Evans
Subject:	Problems during your stay
Sent:	February 16, 3:17 P.M.

信头

Dear Mr. Rock Evans,

名称

　　We understand that you experienced some problems during your recent stay at Millo Hotel. We regret any inconvenience to you and would like to make sure that these problems won't happen again. Could you please describe the problems that you experienced?

正文

Sincerely,

Michael Bull
Manager, Millo Hotel

结尾

　　从上面的图片可以看出，电子邮件主要由四部分构成，分别为：信头、称呼、正文和结尾。信头内容包括发件人、收件人、邮件主题及发送日期；通过信头，可以判断出邮件是由谁发给谁的、邮件的主要内容以及发送的时间；在写作考试第一部分的题目中，提出问题的邮件通常不包含发送日期。而在回复邮件中，信头部分的内容可省略不写，直接写称呼语之后的内容即可。

　　在称呼部分，最常见的方式为Dear+收件人的姓名，如果不清楚收件人的具体姓名或性别，可以使用 Dear Sir or Madam 来代替，也可以使用 To whom it may concern 来表达。

正文部分是邮件的主体，是对主要问题的陈述，正文部分的句子要表达清晰、逻辑缜密，对要点问题做出相应回答。需要注意的是在对要点进行陈述的过程中，考生可以发挥想象，对内容进行相应拓展，最好每个小黑点下面的内容都可以进行分段陈述。

结尾部分包含祝福语、发件人的姓名和职位信息。

二、写作语气

剑桥领思通用英语测评中出现的题目多为朋友间的沟通信函，涉及的内容也多与生活相关，因此在语言的表达上通常使用非正式用语。

考生在平常的学习和日常表达中，需要注意正式用语和非正式用语的表达习惯和两者之间的区别，从而可以在不同的场合进行正确的使用。非正式用语用词比较自由，句型结构比较简单，句子简短直接。体现出发件人和收件人之间试图建立一种随和的、轻松的、亲密的关系。而正式用语在词汇、句子、语法方面都必须严格遵守标准语言的规范，句子较长且语气委婉，所表达的是发件人与收件人之间的一种较正式的关系。

可以比较下面两组句子中正式用语和非正式用语在表达上的区别：

I was wondering if you could help me on this project.（正式用语）

Can you help me on this project?（非正式用语）

Unfortunately, it appears that we are unable to deliver the shipment on time.（正式用语）

We can't deliver the shipment on time.（非正式用语）

下面是对正式用语和非正式用语的对照词汇进行的总结，方便考生进行学习总结：

Informal（非正式用语）	Formal（正式用语）
say sorry	apologize
go up	increase
go down	decrease
set up	establish
look at	examine
blow up	explode
bring about	cause
put off	postpone，delay

Informal（非正式用语）	Formal（正式用语）
rack up	accumulate
make up	fabricate
stand for	represent
find out	discover, ascertain
leave out	omit
point out	indicate
go against	oppose
get in touch with	contact
It's about...	It concerns..., It's in regards to...
need to	（be）required
think about	consider
get	obtain
put up	tolerate
deal with	handle
seem	appear
show	demonstrate, illustrate, portray
start	commence
keep	retain
free	release
get on sb's nerves	bother
ring up	call
show up	arrive
let	permit
fill in	substitute
block	undermine
give the go-ahead, greenlight	authorize

在英文信函的表达中，正式用语和非正式用语的表达方式不尽相同，下面列举一些表达供考生参考：

Informal（非正式用语）	Formal（正式用语）
They did the experiment.	The experiment was carried out/performed.
Thanks for your mail on 10 Mar.	Thank you for your email on the 10th of March.
What do you need?	Please let us know of your requirements.
People use a huge amount of...	People consume a tremendous amount of...
Let me know if we can get together.	Please let me know when you will be available.
Write back soon!	I hope to hear from you at your earliest convenience.
As we discussed this morning, ...	As per our telephone conversation on today's date, ...
I can help you solve this problem.	We can assist in the resolution of this matter.
Don't forget...	I would like to remind you that...
Thanks a lot!	I appreciate your assistance!
Because...	In light of the fact that...
I think...	It is my opinion that...
I need to...	It is necessary for me to...
You don't have to...	It is not necessary for you to...
We recommend...	It is recommended（that）...
Sorry（for）...	Please accept our apologies for...
Another good thing is.../ What's more, ...	Secondly, .../ Besides, ...
What's up?	How do you do?
Nice to meet you.	It is a pleasure to meet you.
As soon as you can	At your earliest convenience...
Worried about you.	Concerned about you.
Firstly, ...	To start with, .../For a start, ...
Say hello to...	Give my regards to...
Heard from her lately?	Have you heard from her lately?
Seen Tom?	Have you seen Tom?
Anna's right.	I agree with my colleague, Anna, that...
You haven't...	We note that you have not...
We want to...	We would like to...
Shall I...?	Would you like me to...?

续表

Informal（非正式用语）	Formal（正式用语）
To think about...	To consider...
To distinguish...	To tell the difference...
This shows that...	This demonstrates...
We've received...	We are in receipt of...
You should revise...	Revision should be done...
It will do you good.	This will be of great benefit to you.

三、开头段和结尾段

开头段

邮件的开头要称呼收件人，这既显得礼貌，也明确提醒收件人，这封邮件是写给他/她的；在写称呼语的时候需要注意使用恰当的称呼。

正式邮件中，对长辈或其他关系不太亲近的收件人通常使用四种称呼表达方式：如果知道收件人的具体姓名，可以用Dear+收件人姓名的方式进行表达，如Dear Jone Smith；如果知道对方的姓氏和性别，可以用Dear+Mr./Ms.+收件人的姓氏的方式进行表达，在这里需要注意，在对女性的称呼上，建议使用Ms.，因为无法确认收件人是否已婚，使用Ms.更为恰当；上述两种表达在知道收件人姓名时使用，当不清楚收件人的具体姓名和性别时，通常使用下面两种表达：Dear Sir or Madam（或Dear Sir/ Madam）和To whom it may concern。

非正式的邮件中，关系较亲近的朋友之间，通常在Hi、Hello或Dear之后加上收件人的名字即可，如"Hi Jan"、"Hello Jenny"或"Dear Kris"，而不是"Hi Jan Brown""Hello Jenny White"或"Dear Kris Patel"。

正式表达	Dear+收件人姓名	在问题邮件中可以找到具体的收件人姓名
	Dear+Mr./ Ms.+收件人的姓氏	在姓的前面加Mr.或Ms.。因为不知道女士是否已婚，因此用Miss或Mrs.称呼女士是不合适的。
	Dear Sir or Madam 或 Dear Sir/ Madam	不知道收件人的具体姓名和性别。
	To whom it may concern	不清楚收件人的具体职位和所在部门，直接翻译为"致相关人员"。
非正式表达	Hi/ Hello/ Dear+收件人名字	关系较亲近的朋友之间，在Hi、Hello或Dear之后加上收件人的名字即可。

在邮件开头部分，除了称呼之外，还会对写信目的进行简要陈述，当涉及不同的目的时，会有一些常用的表达，下面将对一些常用表达方式进行说明。

1. 关于……

"I am writing to…"通常出现在邮件正文的第一句话中，简单直接地表明写邮件的目的。I am writing直译为"我正在写"，但是实际表达的意思为"关于……我写了这封邮件"。in regard to也是告诉对方写信目的最有效的表达方式之一，通常也用于邮件正文的第一句话。在邮件中提到其他问题时，也可以使用这一表达方式，意思为"关于……"，可以和with regard to、as regards、regarding、concerning、about等互相替换使用。

➡ I am writing to+动词（我写这封邮件的目的是……）

I am writing to request a favour. 我写这封邮件的目的是想拜托您一件事。

I am writing to ask for your advice. 我写这封邮件的目的是想请您提建议。

➡ I am writing in+名词+ to（我写这封邮件的目的是……）

I am writing in response to your inquiry. 我写这封邮件的目的是回复您的询问。

I am writing in regard to the appointment. 我写这封邮件是关于预约的事情。

➡ This is in regard to+名词（这封邮件是关于……的）

This is in regard to your e-mail of September 20. 这封邮件是关于您9月20日的来信的。

This is in regard to the party for…. 这封邮件是关于为……举办的派对。

➡ This e-mail is to+动词（这封邮件是为了……）

This e-mail is to inform you of the proposed changes. 这封邮件是为了告诉您一些变更建议。

This e-mail is to notice you about the newly added service of our clinic. 这封邮件是通知您关于我们诊所新增加的服务。

➡ Regarding/ Concerning+名词（关于……）

Regarding the present for…, I suggest we look for some advice on the Internet. 关于给……的礼物，我建议我们在网上寻求一些建议。

Concerning your questions about the delivery service, I think you should call the hotline. 关于您提到的送货服务的问题，我认为您应该拨打热线电话。

2. 表达感谢

在英美文化中，表达感激之情在日常生活中很常见，关系亲近的人之间通常会用"Thanks."或"Thanks a lot."此外还可使用"Thank you very much." "Thank you so

much." "I greatly appreciate...", 以及 "I really appreciate...", 等表达特别的感激之情。
下面是一些表达感谢的常用句型：

➔Thank you/ Thanks for+名词（因某事向您表示感谢）

Thank you for your e-mail. 感谢您的邮件。

Thank you for your kindness. 谢谢您的好意。

Thanks for your e-mail explaining your reason for not attending the party.
感谢您在邮件中对未能参加派对的原因做了说明。

Thanks for the gracious help I received during my trip to the Canada last month.
感谢上个月我在加拿大旅行时您给我的尽心的帮助。

➔Thank you/ Thanks for+-ing（因您做了某事向您表示感谢）

Thank you for getting back to me so fast. 感谢您如此及时地回复我。

Thank you for providing me with the sample. 感谢您为我提供了样品。

Thanks for helping me fix the computer. 感谢您帮我修电脑。

Thanks for telling me about the problems of the newly bought product. 谢谢您告诉我新买的产品的问题。

➔I/ We appreciate+名词（对某事我/ 我们表示感谢）

I appreciate the welcome you gave us last week. 感谢上周您对我们的接待。

We appreciate your interest in the class we provide. 感谢您对我们提供的课程感兴趣。

3. 表达歉意

有很大一部分英语邮件与表达歉意有关。在对歉意的表达中，"I am sorry." 是最常用、最简洁的道歉用语。考生在写道歉类邮件时，需要注意表达要真切，同时在邮件表达中要说明道歉的具体事由，切忌表达不清晰。

➔I apologize for+名词（为某事而道歉）

I apologize for the inconvenience caused to you yesterday. 我为昨天给您带来的不便道歉。

I apologize for my behaviour yesterday. 我为自己昨天的行为道歉。

➔I apologize for+-ing（为做了某事而道歉）

I apologize for not replying sooner. 很抱歉，我没能早点给您回信。

I apologize for not providing detailed information in the advertisement.
我为没有在广告中提供详细信息向您道歉。

➔I am sorry about+名词（为某事而道歉）

I am sorry about the inconvenience my friends may have caused to you.

对于我的朋友可能给您造成的不便，我向您表示歉意。

I am sorry about the late reply. 我很抱歉，这么晚才给您回信。

➡ I am sorry for+-ing（为做某事而道歉）

I am sorry for calling you during your dinner last night. 很抱歉，昨晚在您用餐期间给您打了电话。

I'm sorry for keeping you waiting for so long. 很抱歉让您等了那么长时间。

4. 表达祝贺

当对对方的乔迁、结婚、升职等喜事表示祝贺时，邮件通常要以congratulations这个单词开头，或者也可以把该词放在句子中间。该词还可以做邮件的标题。

➡ Congratulations!（祝贺!）

Congratulations! You have a healthy baby boy. 祝贺你! 生了个健康的男孩。

Congratulations! I heard the news. 祝贺你! 我听说那个消息了。

➡ Congratulations on...（祝贺……）

Congratulations on your birthday! 祝贺你的生日!

Congratulations on your promotion! 祝贺你晋升!

➡ I/ We would like to congratulate you on...（我/ 我们要祝贺你……）

I would like to congratulate you on moving to the new house. 我要祝贺你搬到新家。

We would like to congratulate you on the great speech you made for us yesterday. 我们要祝贺你昨天为我们做的精彩演讲。

结尾段

根据收件人的不同，邮件中可使用不同的结束语来表达收件人和发件人之间的亲疏关系。下面将举例说明不同的关系中应该使用的结束语。

（1）Thanks./ Thank you.

Thanks.偏随和，而Thank you比较正式，常用于商务场合。

（2）Yours./ Yours truly./ Truly.

"Yours./ Yours truly." 和 "Truly." 这三种表达均可在日常交往中使用，算是一种比较私人的结束语，但同时也可以体现出发件人的礼貌。一般用于之前见过面的对象。

（3）Best./ Best Wishes.

日常交往或者商务场合都可以用，是一种礼貌的表达方式。对朋友和陌生人都可以用。

（4）Sincerely./ Sincerely yours./ Yours sincerely.

在日常交往或更正式的信件中是标准的信件结束用语。"Sincerely."是使用范围最广的一种结束语，无论日常和正式通信都可以使用。如果不确定怎么结尾署名，则可以使用"Sincerely."。

（5）Cheers.

一种较为随意的结尾，一般在与好友通信时使用。也可以用于和同事间的通信。

（6）Take care.

适用于朋友之间的通信。

四、主体段

邮件主体段包含电子邮件的核心内容，是邮件的关键。在写作的时候需要注意以下几点：

1. 对邮件中提出的问题进行相应的回复，通常一个段落回应一个要点；
2. 拓展观点，充实内容。第一部分的电子邮件至少要有50个单词，所以需要尽可能多地拓展观点。一些常见的拓展观点的方法包括：提供理由、添加细节、提供对比；
3. 不要出现语法错误。

此外，为了使句子连接更紧凑、段落更紧密，考生还需要掌握一些衔接词，用于衔接段落中的观点，下面是一些常用的衔接词。

1. 表示时间的衔接词

词汇	释义
before	在……以前
after	在……之后
since	从……以来
next	紧接着；随后
during	在……期间
at the same time	同时
finally	最后

2. 表示顺序、程度的衔接词

词汇	释义
firstly	第一；首先

续表

词汇	释义
secondly	第二；其次
finally	终于；最终
lastly	最后一点；最后
the second reason is	第二个原因是
to begin with	首先；起初
most importantly	最重要的是
basically	基本上；从本质上来说
one reason is primarily	一个原因主要是
the first reason is essentially	第一个原因本质上是
another reason is principally	另一个原因主要是

3. 表示比较、对象的衔接词

词汇	释义
similar to A	与A相似；和A相同
similarly	相似地；类似
also	而且；此外；也
at the same time	同时
in the same way	以同样的方式
likewise	同样地；类似地
even though	虽然；即使
unlike	不像；和……不同
otherwise	否则；不然；除此以外
in contrast to	相比之下
on the other hand	另一方面；换句话说

4. 表示原因、结果的衔接词

词汇	释义
for this reason	为此；由于这个原因
since	因为；由于
as a result	所以；结果（是）

词汇	释义
due to	由于；因为
consequently	因此；所以
because	因为；由于
because of	因为；由于；基于
therefore	因此；所以；因而
owing to	由于；因为；多亏
so that	以便；因此

5. 表示说明的衔接词

词汇	释义
in other words	换句话说；也就是说；换言之
to illustrate	举例而言；说明
to explain	说明
that is	也就是说；换言之
for instance/ example	例如；举例说
such as	比如；诸如
to clarify	说得更明白些

6. 表示追加说明内容的衔接词

词汇	释义
in addition	除此之外；另外
moreover	再者；此外；而且
besides	此外；除了
similarly	相似地；类似地
furthermore	此外；而且；与此同时
what's more	另外；更重要的是；而且
additionally	此外
in fact	事实上；实际上

　　主体段部分除了上述衔接词外，还有一些常用的表达句式，下面将对常用的句式进行简要说明：

1. 表示遗憾

　　英文表达中，sorry 除了可以表达歉意外，还可用于对对方所发生的事情礼貌性地表示遗憾，一般在对话或书面表达中比较常用。通常我们认为"I'm sorry..."只表示道歉。其实在英语国家，"I'm sorry..."还通常表示遗憾。电子邮件中表示遗憾常用的句型如下：

➡I'm sorry（that）+从句（很遗憾……）

I'm sorry that you have to leave. 很遗憾您要离开了。

I'm sorry that you can't join us. 很遗憾您不能跟我们一起。

➡I'm sorry to+动词（很遗憾……）

I'm sorry to see you go. 很遗憾看着你离开。

I'm sorry to hear the news. 听到那个消息我很遗憾。

➡I'm sorry, but...（很遗憾，但是……）

I'm sorry, but I can't authorize it. 很遗憾，但是我不能授权。

I'm sorry, but that is not possible. 很遗憾，但是那是不可能的。

➡Regretfully, ...（遗憾的是，……）

Regretfully, we have to decline your kind invitation. 遗憾的是，我们不得不拒绝您的盛情邀请。

Regretfully, I won't be able to attend the meeting. 遗憾的是，我将无法参加会议。

➡Unfortunately, ...（不幸的是，……；遗憾的是，……）

Unfortunately, you can't enjoy free shipping service. 遗憾的是，您无法享受免费的运送服务。

Unfortunately, it rained all day. 遗憾的是，雨下了一整天。

2. 表示自己希望或者要做某事

　　当表示自己希望做什么事情或者要做什么事情时，I would 是最合适、最郑重的表达用语，电子邮件的写作中也经常使用到。与之类似的另一种表达方式是 I will，但是I will 多少会给人一种强硬的感觉，因此大多数情况下用would 更委婉、恰当。

➡I would be+形容词（我会……）

I would be grateful for your information. 我会感谢您提供的信息。

I would be honored to attend the banquet. 我将很荣幸去参加宴会。

➡I would+动词（我会……）

I would appreciate your help. 我会感谢您的帮助。

I would talk to him directly. 我会直接跟他说。

➡I would like to+动词（我想……）

I would like to thank you for your help. 我想感谢您的帮助。

I would like to ask a favour. 我想请您帮个忙。

3. 表示委婉地询问"可以……吗？"

简单地向别人请求一件事时，通常在could后加主语（I、you、we），然后再加动词。向亲近关系的人请求可以用can来代替could。例如"Could you send me... ?"可以用"Can you send me... ?"来代替，"Could I ask... ?"也可以用"Can I ask... ?"来代替。当请求对方给予许可或协助时，可以用"Would it be...?"这一句式，它表达的语气跟"Could... ?"类似。"Would it be possible for me to... ?"可以用"Could I... ?"来代替，"Would it be possible for you to...?"也可以用"Could you... ?"来代替。

➡Could you+动词（您可以……吗？）

Could you send me an e-mail? 您可以给我发一封电子邮件吗？

Could you call me tomorrow? 明天您能给我打电话吗？

➡Could I+动词（我可以……吗？）

Could I get an extension on the holiday? 我可以延长一下假期吗？

Could I call you tomorrow to discuss the party for ...? 明天我可以给您打电话商议一下……的聚会吗？

➡Could we +动词（我们……，怎么样？）

Could we meet tomorrow? 我们明天见面，怎么样？

Could we postpone the appointment? 我们把预约推迟一下，怎么样？

➡Would it be possible to+动词（可以……吗？）

Would it be possible to turn it in tomorrow? 可以明天上交吗？

Would it be possible to get the feedback earlier? 可以早一点得到反馈吗？

➡Would it be possible for me/ you to+动词（我/ 您可以……吗？）

Would it be possible for me to get more information? 我可以得到更多的信息吗？

Would it be possible for you to leave a message for her? 您能给她留言吗？

➡Would it be okay if I+动词过去式（我……，行吗？）

Would it be okay if I went with you? 我跟您一起去，行吗？

Would it be okay if I called you tomorrow at 10? 我明天10点给您打电话，行吗？

➡Would you mind if I+动词过去式（您介意我……吗？）

Would you mind if I took a day off? 您介意我请一天假吗？

Would you mind if I asked you several questions? 您介意我问您几个问题吗？

➡ Would you be able to+动词（您能……吗？）

Would you be able to come over on Saturday night? 您星期六晚上能过来吗？

Would you be able to do me a big favour? 您能帮我个大忙吗？

➡ If possible, ...（如果可以的话，……）

If possible, I would like to come by tomorrow. 如果可以的话，我想明天过来。

If possible, please tell me the result by this evening. 如果可以的话，请在今晚之前告诉我结果。

4. 表达高兴

告知对方好消息时，为了表达自己的喜悦之情，一般使用 "I am/ We are pleased/ happy to..." 或 "It is my/ our pleasure to..." 或 "I/ We would be glad to..." 或 "It would be my/ our pleasure to..." 这些句型来表示自己乐意做某事。

➡ I am/ We are pleased/ happy to+动词（我/ 我们很高兴……）

I am pleased to hear that you enjoyed our preparation. 听说您喜欢我们所做的准备，我很高兴。

We are pleased to see the problem settled so quickly. 我们很高兴看到问题这么快就被解决了。

I am happy to tell you that our community is going to build an activity center for the old.

我很高兴地告诉您，我们社区将为老年人建立一个活动中心。

We are happy to be able to accommodate your request. 我们很高兴接受您的请求。

➡ It is my/ our pleasure to+动词（我/ 我们很高兴……）

It is my pleasure to accept your invitation. 我很高兴接受您的邀请。

It is our pleasure to note that China has made great progress in economy. 我们很高兴地看到，中国的经济已经有了很大的发展。

➡ I/ We would be glad to+动词（我/ 我们很乐意……）

I would be glad to join your club. 我很乐意加入你的俱乐部。

We would be glad to attend your wedding. 我们很开心能参加你的婚礼。

➡ It would be my/ our pleasure to+动词（我/ 我们很乐意……）

It would be my pleasure to give you some advice. 我很高兴能给你一些建议。

It would be our pleasure to reserve the hotel rooms for you. 我们很乐意为您预

订酒店房间。

5. 表达某事是按照或根据什么而得来的

提到之前的说明、讨论或请求时，英语中通常用as短语，即根据as短语中的内容说出自己的行动或结果。

➡ As+主语+mentioned，...（正如……所提到的，……）

As I mentioned in my last e-mail, distance education is now growing at an incredible rate.

正如我在上一封邮件中所提到的那样，远程教育现在正以惊人的速度发展。

As we mentioned earlier, the best rewards are thought out and planned.

正如我们先前提到的那样，最好的奖励既要出人意料，又要合情合理。

➡ As+主语+requested，...（根据……的要求，……）

As you requested, I'm attaching the file in MS Word. 根据您的要求，我添加了用MS Word格式做的附件。

As Roger requested, the party will be at his home. 按照罗杰的要求，这次聚会将在他家里举行。

➡ As we discussed，...（正如我们所商讨的那样，……）

As we discussed, my team will prepare the drawings. 正如我们所商讨的那样，我的团队将准备图纸。

As we discussed last week, I am scheduled to arrive in London this Friday. 正如我们上周所商讨的那样，我计划这周五到达伦敦。

➡ As+动词（按照……/ 就像……）

As laid out in my last memo, the new store hours will be from 8 a.m. to 11 p.m.

就像我在上次的备忘录上所写的那样，商店新的营业时间是从上午8点到晚上11点。

As Daniel said yesterday morning during our brief meeting, we will send out the press release tomorrow afternoon.

就像丹尼尔在昨天上午的碰头会上所说的那样，我们要在明天下午把新闻稿发出去。

6. 请求或要求

如果不是特别亲近的关系，要求对方做某件事时通常要用please。中国人通常认为please相当于含有拜托或恳求语气的"一定"或"请求"，但是在英语国家，该词通常作为一种礼貌用语而被人们广泛使用。

➔ Please+动词（请……）

Please call me if you have any question. 如果您有任何问题，请给我打电话。

Please forward me the information by tomorrow. 请在明天之前把信息发给我。

➔ I/ We ask that you+动词（我/ 我们希望你/ 您……）

I ask that you send me the hotel address as soon as possible. 我希望你尽快把酒店地址发给我。

We ask that you contact us to confirm the date of meeting. 我们希望您跟我们联系以确认会面日期。

➔ I/ We request that +从句（我/ 我们要求……）

I request that the borrowed tools be returned in time when you finish using them. 我要求借用的工具在用完之后必须及时归还。

We request that this matter be discussed in your next meeting. 我们要求在你们下一次的会议上讨论这个问题。

五、常见话题

领思写作考试中，第一部分的题目通常要求考生在回复的邮件中对某一日常话题进行回复，因此考生在平时需要积累常见的话题，并掌握一定的回答思路，从而可以在考试时应答自如。这里将对一些常见的话题及相应的回答思路进行说明。

1. 聚会
- 生日聚会
- 为朋友举办聚会（归来/ 离去）
- 为新来的邻居举办欢迎活动
- 烧烤晚会

聚会是经常出现的一个话题，涉及的内容主要包含上面四个方面，下面将对经常问到的问题和相应的回答思路进行说明。

➔ 跟聚会相关的常见问题

✦ 聚会开始的时间 The starting time of the party

✦ 聚会地点 The place where the party is held

✦ 建议带去聚会的食物/ 礼物 Suggested food/ gifts to the party

✦ 建议在聚会上进行的活动 Suggested activities at the party

✦ 参加聚会的人员 People to attend the party

✦ 收到的礼物 Gifts received

✦ 说明你所在国家的人们如何庆祝生日 Explain how people in your country celebrate their birthdays

✦ 建议在该区域进行一项户外/室内活动 Suggest an outdoor/ indoor activity in the area.

➡ 上述问题相关回答思路

✦ 聚会尽量安排在周末

It would be best if the party takes place during the weekend because that's when most people are free.

Perhaps Saturday night would make the most sense, since some of us need to sleep earlier on Sundays.

✦ 实用的礼物

Something with practical use will be a good choice.

✦ 唱生日歌、吹蜡烛、赠送礼物、做互动小游戏、邀请朋友过来做游戏和聚餐、在野外聚餐

sing birthday songs

blow out candles

give gifts

do interactive games

invite friends over to play games and have dinner together

have a picnic outside

✦ 将聚会安排在有趣的地方

游乐场：playground

特殊项目的场馆：climbing centre/ gym centre

手工工作室：workshop for making clay/ drawing studio

2. 介绍家乡 ⎰ 旅游景点介绍
推荐适合旅行的交通工具
推荐最好的参观时间
旅行应该避开一年中的哪段时间
推荐适合的住宿地
从机场到市中心的最佳线路
推荐一些可以做的事情

跟朋友介绍自己家乡的风景名胜、自然历史和气候特点在领思写作考试中也是经常

出现的，尤其多见于异国朋友之间。上面列出的内容是题目要求中常出现的问题，考生在准备的过程中可重点关注。

➡ 旅游景点介绍

✦ The old tower has a long history of 1,500 years.

✦ Our town is an old city dating back to the late seventeenth century.

✦ There are many places of interest, such as...

✦ The beautiful town is located along the shore of the lake.

➡ 推荐适合旅行的交通工具

✦ We can ride bikes around the sea.

✦ With convenient transportation, bus and taxi are both good choices.

✦ You can enjoy the beautiful scenery along the way on foot.

➡ 推荐最好的参观时间

✦ Spring is a good choice as everything comes back to life in spring and the weather gets warmer.

✦ The snow in winter is more beautiful than the flowers in spring.

✦ Autumn is a harvest season.

➡ 旅行应该避开哪段时间

✦ Midweek is a good time to travel to avoid the crowd.

✦ Please avoid this period of time.

➡ 推荐适合的住宿地

✦ To get away from noise and pollution in the city and take a vacation in the place where there is peace and solitude is a great choice to me.

✦ away from all the hustle and bustle of the city

✦ close to mother nature

✦ peaceful evenings/ peace and quiet of the country/ very peaceful/ calm

✦ no bad traffic

➡ 从机场到市中心的最佳线路

✦ There's an airport bus, which is very convenient.

✦ A taxi will cost you an arm and a leg, so the subway is a good choice.

➡ 推荐一些可以做的事情

✦ If you ever got a chance to pass a farm with peach trees and tomatoes, you can smell the freshness of the fruit.

✦ In summer, there are a whole lot of activities that you can do, like going to the beach, just lying on the beach or going ahead and doing some water skiing.

3. 描述课程 ┤ 介绍课程中心新开的课程
对广告中的课程进行回复
对课程进行推荐

日常生活中会涉及各类培训课程，其中包括与文化相关的课程，也包含各类体育和艺术课程，在写作考试的题目中常常涉及对上述问题的回复。

介绍课程中心新开的课程 ┤ 课程开始时间（艺术课/ 体育课）
课程时长
上课时需要带的材料
对上课形式的选择（一对一/ 小组课）

➔ 课程开始时间

✦ Course starts on August 20.

✦ Courses are available every Wednesday afternoon from 1:00 to 2:00.

✦ The next class is on Sunday at ten o'clock in the morning.

➔ 课程时长

✦ The course lasts for one hour every time.

➔ 上课时需要带的材料

✦ Take your notebook and pen to attend the class.

✦ Please wear sports clothes to class.

➔ 对上课形式的选择

✦ One-on-one lessons are more efficient.

✦ Group classes are more active.

对广告中的课程进行回复 ┤ 说明自己想要参加的课程
解释对这门课程感兴趣的原因
对课程相关事宜进行提问

➔ 说明自己想要参加的课程

✦ I am very interested in music./ I am deeply intrigued by music.

➔ 解释对这门课程感兴趣的原因

✦ If you are intrigued by something, especially something strange, it will interest you and you will want to know more about it.

➡ 对课程相关事宜进行提问

✦ May I know the education background of the teachers?

✦ Will there be relevant certificates after the course?

对课程进行推荐 ⎰ 对相关课程进行推荐
　　　　　　　⎱ 说明推荐的理由
　　　　　　　　 说明参观课程中心的最佳时间

➡ 对相关课程进行推荐

✦ I think you should try the beginners' class.

➡ 说明推荐的理由

✦ Classes for beginners are fun and not too challenging.

✦ The coaches here are very experienced.

➡ 说明参观课程中心的最佳时间

✦ It's best to go during the weekdays after 8 a.m..

✦ There are courses in the weekends. You can have a visit and experience the course during that time.

4. 对自己的情况进行介绍 ⎰ 基本信息（姓名、年龄、居住地）
　　　　　　　　　　 业余爱好
　　　　　　　　　　 家庭成员
　　　　　　　　　　 目前职业或就读学校
　　　　　　　　　　 喜欢的食物
　　　　　　　　　　 未来的职业规划

　　在写作考试第一部分的题目中，对自己的情况进行介绍是比较常见的内容，考生对这部分内容也比较熟悉，在遇到类似题目时考生需要认真思考，组织好语言，同时做好内容的扩展。

➡ 基本信息

✦ My name is... and I'm 18 years old.

✦ I'm Li Ming. My English name is Tony, and you can call me Tony.

✦ I am twenty years of age.

➡ 业余爱好

✦ I've always liked listening to inspiring speeches.

✦ My hobbies are swimming and tennis.

✦ I love listening to music, too.

✦ I am/ get excited about surfing the Internet.

✦ I have a passion for American movies.

✦ playing football/ watching TV/ growing flowers/ eating food/ playing basketball/ traveling/ reading/ writing

➡ 家庭成员

✦ I've got 2 brothers, Daniel and Wilson.

✦ There are six people in my family. They are my grandfather, my grandmother, my father, my mother, my sister and I.

✦ I have a big family. There are five people in my family. They are my father, my mother, my grandparents and I.

✦ I have a happy family with father, mother, brother and I.

➡ 目前职业或就读学校

✦ I am a student. I'm studying Engineering at the university.

✦ I have graduated for two years and now work in a multinational company.

✦ I'm a student majoring in Electronic Engineering at the provincial university.

➡ 喜欢的食物

✦ Dumplings are the most traditional food and I like dumplings.

✦ Hamburger is a kind of fast food from western countries, and it is very convenient and delicious.

✦ My favourite food is vegetables.

➡ 未来的职业规划

✦ It has been one of my dreams to become a/ an···

✦ Setting career goals is the core of career planning.

✦ In determining a career goal, action has become the key link.

5. 假期安排 ┤ 说明假期去了哪里/ 推荐一个假期一起出去放松的地方
说明假期进行了哪些活动
邀请朋友一起度假
跟朋友讲述假期经历

➡ 说明假期去了哪里/ 推荐一个假期一起出去放松的地方

✦ I spent the summer holiday in my grandma's home.

✦ Last winter, I went to the capital city of China, Beijing.

➡ 说明假期进行了哪些活动

✦ play basketball/ go swim/ go shopping/ play Ping-Pong/ play games/ do holiday homework

✦ camp/ go skiing/ go hiking

➔ 邀请朋友一起度假

✦ I really look forward to seeing you after such a long while.

✦ It would be great if you could come and have a holiday with us.

✦ I guarantee that we can spice up our holiday.

✦ You have my word that the trip is going to be great.

✦ Let us know when you can come and we will make the arrangements.

✦ You haven't been here for a while, so this is a chance to catch up with your old friends.

➔ 跟朋友讲述假期经历

✦ I really had a busy and happy winter holiday.

✦ I have a great time during the winter holiday, because I enjoy myself as well as focus on my study.

✦ This year's summer vacation was the most enjoyable. I spent fifteen days helping my grandparents do farm work in the countryside, where I saw mountain fields covered with green plants.

✦ If you ask me what my favourite summer holiday will be like, traveling around the world is the only answer.

6. 音乐相关 { 音乐歌曲 / 音乐会相关内容

音乐是人们生活中一个重要的元素，起着调剂生活的作用。在写作考试中，与音乐相关的题目也很常见。

音乐歌曲 { 喜欢的音乐有哪些 / 最喜欢的乐队有哪些 / 说明收藏乐队专辑的数量 / 听音乐的时间段

➔ 喜欢的音乐有哪些

✦ folk song 民歌

✦ Rhythm and Blues 节奏布鲁斯

✦ Rock and Roll 摇滚乐

✦ Rap 说唱音乐

✦ Pop 流行音乐

➔ 最喜欢的乐队有哪些

✦The Beatles 甲壳虫乐队

✦The Rolling Stones 滚石乐队

✦Queen 皇后乐队

➔ 说明收藏乐队专辑的数量

✦I like this band and have collected all their albums since their debut.

➔ 听音乐的时间段

✦ when the pressure is high

✦ when a relax is needed

✦ during the bathing

✦ while eating alone

音乐会相关 ⎰ 说明音乐会的地点
⎱ 邀请朋友一起去听音乐会
    解释为什么这场音乐会受欢迎

➔ 说明音乐会的地点

✦ gymnasiums 体育馆

✦ concert halls 音乐厅

✦ multi-functional hall of the university 大学的多功能厅

➔ 邀请朋友一起去听音乐会

✦ We are very honored to invite you to the concert we will hold on Saturday.

✦ Could you go to the central park with me to enjoy the concert provided by the Flowers Band?

➔ 解释为什么这场音乐会受欢迎

✦ Two famous violinists are taking part in the show, so it must be very exciting.

✦ The concert was performed like inspiration.

Day 3　提分篇——常见任务类型讲解

一、提供建议

　　根据回复邮件的不同内容，领思写作第一部分电子邮件的任务类型可分为提供建议、情况说明以及其他这三种类型。提供建议是最常见的一种类型，主要形式为发件人就某件事情询问收件人的看法或意见，并希望收件人对此事提供建议。这一类型的题目所涉及的内容多与生活相关，考生在平时的练习中可以多积累相关问题的回答思路和技巧，下面将对提供建议类邮件进行相关说明。

（一）常用表达

　　提供建议类的邮件中，题目中通常会要求在回复的邮件中对某件事提供建议，常用的表达为：

recommend...to...

suggest a gift/ routine to...

suggest a good way to...

suggest a good...for...

suggest a time when you can...

offer to help...

offer to find out more information about...

recommend some things for...

　　观察了上面的句型之后考生会发现，在接下来的邮件中需要提供某件事情的解决方案或建议合适的时间来做某事。在有些题目中，还会要求考生对自己提出的建议进行进一步的解释说明，常见的表达如下：

explain when would be the best time for...

say why you think...

explain when a good time would be to...

explain why you think...

explain why your...is/ are good

考生在写回复邮件的时候，首先需要在第一段表达自己收到邮件时的感受，同时回指先前的联系或者对写信事由进行说明，这里常用到的表达有：

Many thanks for your kind letter which reached me yesterday.

I was so pleased to receive your letter.

Your kind letter gives me much pleasure.

Thank you for your letter of/ about...

Thank you for your letter dated...

With reference to your letter of/ about...

Further to your offer letter of...

In reply to your inquiry of...

I'm writing to explain...

主体段部分，考生需要对主要问题进行回复。建议每个段落回应题目中的一个要点，下面为一些常用的表达：

I think that...would work best for everyone.

Here I would like to explain that...

There are several reasons for...

I think that it would be best if...

The reason why...is that...

As for the..., I think...is better.

I believe that, ...is a good choice for...

结尾部分，考生需要进行礼貌性的回复，表达期待相见及保持联系等：

Thank you very much!

Look forward to your early reply.

Look forward to hearing from you soon.

Can't wait to see you soon!

（二）典型例题及详解

1.

You have received this email from your classmate Daniel.

> From: Daniel
>
> Did you know that Bella will leave soon? I think we should have a going-away party for her in the following week. Would you be willing to plan it with me? I'm not sure if the party should take place during a weekday or the weekend. And have you got any ideas about a good going-away present for her?
>
> Daniel

Write an email to your classmate Daniel:

- agree to help plan the party with Daniel
- say why you think the party should take place during the weekend
- suggest a good going-away present for Bella.

Write at least 50 words.

通过观察上面的邮件可以发现，这是同学之间的一封邮件，两个人共同认识的一位同学要离开，发件人询问收件人是否可以帮忙组织一次聚会，并对临别礼物提供建议。

邮件列出了三点任务要求，考生需要从这几个方面进行回答，分别是对同意帮助组织聚会进行肯定回答，对在周末举办聚会的理由进行说明，同时为临别礼物提供建议。

下面是一则范文：

Hi Daniel,

How's it going? Yes, I've heard that Bella is moving away soon, which is pretty sad. I definitely agree that we should throw a going-away party for her. She's been such a great friend, and we'll all miss her a lot.

写作考试第一部分的邮件多为朋友间的信函往来，话题也与生活相关，因此要使用非正式的文体。这篇范文中，开头的称呼语使用的是"Hi+名字"，因为发件人和收件人之间为同学关系，关系较亲密，Hi的使用体现出了这种同学之间较亲密随意的关系，同时称呼语后面直接跟的是收件人的名字，而不是全名。

开头段中，发件人首先对收件人进行了问候，然后对第一个问题进行了回复，即

"I definitely agree that we should throw a going-away party for her." 对原邮件中提出的问题进行了肯定回答。

I would be happy to plan the party with you, but I'm afraid you'll have to do most of the work because I'm not too experienced at planning parties. Maybe I can take care of contacting people, while you handle the major planning.

邮件正文第二段中，作者对第一个要点进行了详细的说明，即很乐意帮忙组织聚会，但在组织聚会方面没有太多经验，可以负责联系参加聚会的人员。

I think that it would be best if the party takes place during the weekend because that's when most people are free. Perhaps Saturday night would make the most sense, since some of us need to sleep earlier on Sunday's.

邮件正文第三段中，作者对第二个要点进行了回复，说明聚会安排在周末的原因。同时说明了将聚会安排在周六晚上是最好的选择，并说明了这样安排的原因。

As for a good going-away present, I would suggest you buy something that Bella will need at her new apartment. I heard she's moving to the south where it's hot, so maybe you could buy her a mini fan. Sorry if it doesn't seem like a great idea, but it's all I can think of for now.

在主体部分的第四段，作者对第三个要点进行了回复。作者在这里陈述了自己的观点并对观点进行了解释说明，可以说是有理有据。

邮件最后部分作者通过委婉地表达："Sorry if it doesn't seem like a great idea, but it's all I can think of for now." 避免自己的观点与发件人的意见不一致。

Anyway, let me know your thoughts on everything!

结尾部分，作者进行了礼貌性回复。

Cheers,

Gerald

最后是祝福语和发件人姓名。在这里作者使用了Cheers，体现出朋友间比较随意的感觉。写完整篇文章后，需要检查一下字数是否达到50个单词，如果不够50个单词需要再增加一些内容。在保证字数的情况下，还需要注意时间问题。作文部分的总时间是45分钟，分配到第一部分的时间是15分钟，如果第一部分的时间超过15分钟，则会影响到第二部分的写作。

完整的范文如下：

Hi Daniel,

How's it going? Yes, I've heard that Bella is moving away soon, which is pretty sad. I definitely agree that we should throw a going-away party for her. She's been such a great friend, and we'll all miss her a lot.

I would be happy to plan the party with you, but I'm afraid you'll have to do most of the work because I'm not too experienced at planning parties. Maybe I can take care of contacting people, while you handle the major planning.

I think that it would be best if the party takes place during the weekend because that's when most people are free. Perhaps Saturday night would make the most sense, since some of us need to sleep earlier on Sunday's.

As for a good going-away present, I would suggest you buy something that Bella will need at her new apartment. I heard she's moving to the south where it's hot, so maybe you could buy her a mini fan. Sorry if it doesn't seem like a great idea, but it's all I can think of for now.

Anyway, let me know your thoughts on everything!

Cheers,
Gerald

范文翻译:

> 嗨，丹尼尔：
>
> 最近怎么样？是的，我听说贝拉很快就要搬走了，这真让人难过。我们应该为她举办一个欢送会，这一点我完全同意。她是个很好的朋友，我们都会很想念她的。
>
> 我很乐意和你一起策划这次聚会，但恐怕大部分工作都得由你来做，因为我在策划聚会方面不太有经验。也许我可以负责联系参加聚会的人，而你负责主要的策划。
>
> 我认为聚会最好在周末举办，因为那时候大多数人都有空。也许周六晚上是最合适的，因为我们中的一些人需要在周日晚上早点睡觉。
>
> 至于一份好的送别礼物，我建议你买一个贝拉在新公寓需要的东西。我听说她要搬到南方去，那里很热，也许你可以给她买个迷你风扇。如果这看起来不像是一个好主意，我很抱歉，但这是我目前能想到的全部了。
>
> 不管怎样，告诉我你对每件事情的想法！
>
> 祝愉快，
>
> 杰拉尔德

➤ 重点词汇及短语

1. pretty [ˈprɪti] *adv.* 很；相当
2. definitely [ˈdefɪnətli] *adv.* 确定；明显地；明确地
3. miss [mɪs] *vt.* 怀念；思念
4. experienced [ɪkˈspɪəriənst] *adj.* 有经验的；熟练的
5. handle [ˈhændl] *vt.* 处理，应付（局势、人、工作或感情）
6. apartment [əˈpɑːtmənt] *n.* 公寓套房
7. fan [fæn] *n.* 风扇
8. take care of 负责；处理
9. take place 发生；举行

➤重点句型及例句

1. throw a party 举办派对、酒会等

例：Why not throw a party for your friends?

为什么不为你的朋友办个派对呢?

2. it would be best to... 最好……

例：It would be best to ask Jane about that.

关于那件事，最好是问珍妮。

3. make the most sense 最有意义

例：What jobs make the most sense for a robot?

什么工作对机器人最有意义?

2.

You have received this email from a friend who you went to college with.

Do you remember we talked about going away on holiday together for a week this summer? I think we should get out of the city and go somewhere relaxing. Have you got any ideas about where we could go and when?

Email me back with your ideas.

Hugs,

Linda

Write an email to Linda:

• suggest a relaxing place to go on holiday together

• explain when a good time would be to go

• offer to find out more information about the holiday

Write at least 50 words.

通过观察上面的邮件可发现，邮件中并没有写称呼，只是结尾处有发件人的姓名。根据邮件内容可推测出这是关系较亲密的朋友间的邮件往来，邮件的内容是关于夏天出去度假一周的事情。

邮件下方列出了三点任务要求，分别为推荐一个放松的地方一起度假、说明什么时间是去度假的好时机以及提供有关假期的更多信息。考生在作答的时候需要根据这三点任务要求来组织内容。

下面是一则范文：

Hi Linda,

Thanks for your email. So nice to hear from you. I was just thinking about our holiday.

通过提出问题的邮件可以发现发件人和收件人之间亲密的关系，在回复的邮件中，作者使用了较亲密的称呼，作者使用了Hi加收件人的名字，Hi的使用体现出了这种朋友之间较亲密随意的关系，同时称呼语后面直接跟的是收件人的名字，而不是全名。

问候语中，作者首先对收到邮件表示感谢，同时对发件人提到的问题进行了回应，即"I was just thinking about our holiday"。

I totally agree about getting away from the city. Why don't we go to the coast? There are some fantastic beaches near Trieste. We could get the train there and hire a car. How about renting a beach cabin?

邮件正文第一段中，作者对发件人提出的问题进行了肯定回复，即"I totally agree about getting away from the city."接下来提出了自己的建议，"Why don't we go to the coast？"并说明了自己的理由"There are some fantastic beaches near Trieste. We could get the train there and hire a car."这段内容是对题目要求中第一个要点的回复。

I think May would be best. The week beginning with Saturday 22nd would be good. I've got a lot on at work in June and I think the coast will be busy later in the summer.

邮件正文第二段中，作者对题目要求中第二个要点进行了回复，说明了去度假的最好时间是什么时候。同时在这段中，作者对自己的理由进行了说明"I've got a lot on at work in June and I think the coast will be busy later in the summer."做到了有理有据。

Shall I go online and find out the information about beach cabins? Would you like me to check out car hire prices, too?

邮件正文最后一段是对第三个要点的回复，作者在这里提到是否需要上网查一下海滩小屋或者查一下租车的价格，同时这也是对第一个要点中提到的内容的回应。

Email me back and tell me what you think.

结尾部分，作者表示希望收到收件人的回信。

Amelia

最后是发件人姓名。

　　这封邮件对题目要求中的三个要点分别进行了回复，内容也符合逻辑，同时字数也达到了规定要求，超过了50个单词，是一篇合格的文章。考生在写作的过程中，既要保证内容的逻辑性，也要确保字数满足要求。

　　完整的范文如下：

Hi Linda,

Thanks for your email. So nice to hear from you. I was just thinking about our holiday.

I totally agree about getting away from the city. Why don't we go to the coast? There are some fantastic beaches near Trieste. We could get the train there and hire a car. How about renting a beach cabin?

I think May would be best. The week beginning with Saturday 22nd would be good. I've got a lot on at work in June and I think the coast will be busy later in the summer.

Shall I go online and find out the information about beach cabins? Would you like me to check out car hire prices, too?

Email me back and tell me what you think.

Amelia

范文翻译：

嗨，琳达：

感谢你的电子邮件。很高兴收到你的来信。我刚好在想我们的假期。

我完全同意离开这个城市。我们为什么不去海边？里雅斯特附近有一些很棒的海滩。我们可以乘火车去那里，然后租辆车。租个海滩小屋怎么样？

我觉得五月最好。从星期六22号开始的那一周就好了。六月份我有很多工作要做，我想夏天晚些时候海边会有很多人。

我要不要上网查一下海滩小屋的相关信息？你想让我也查一下租车价格吗？

回信给我，告诉我你的想法。

阿梅利亚

➤ 重点词汇及短语

1. totally [ˈtəʊtəli] *adv.* 完全；全部地
2. coast [kəʊst] *n.* 海岸；海滨
3. fantastic [fænˈtæstɪk] *adj.* 极好的；极大的；奇异的
4. rent [rent] *vt.* 租用；租借
5. hire [ˈhaɪə（r）] *vt.* 租用；租借
6. cabin [ˈkæbɪn] *n.* 小木屋；（船上的）小舱
7. get away 离开，脱身

➤ 重点句型及例句

1. think about 考虑，打算（做某事）

例：What did you think about the idea?

你认为这个想法怎么样？

2. Why don't we... 我们为什么不……?

例：Why don't we close up and go out for lunch?

我们为什么不关上门出去吃顿午饭？

二、情况说明

　　情况说明在领思写作考试中也是极为常见的一种题目类型，主要是对朋友和同事在邮件中提到的问题进行解释说明，其中通常还会包含对某一事件或问题的看法或建议。考生在平时需要多加练习，下面将对情况说明类邮件进行相关说明。

（一）常用表达

　　在提出问题的邮件中，邮件下面的写作要求中通常会包含如下内容：

tell...

say when/ why...

explain why you can't...

describe how you...

　　看到上面的句型，考生应该了解到，这里需要对某种情况和原因进行解释说明，在个别题目中，还需要考生提出建议或看法，常用的表达如下：

suggest how you can...

suggest a gift/ routine for...

recommend...to...

　　考生在写回复邮件的时候，首先需要在第一段回指先前的联系或者对写信事由进行说明，这里常用到的表达有：

Thank you for your letter of/ about...

Thank you for your letter dated...

With reference to your letter of/ about...

Further to your offer letter of...

In reply to your inquiry of...

I'm writing to explain...

　　主体段部分，考生需要对主要问题进行回复。建议每个段落回应题目中的一个要点，下面为一些常用的表达：

Here I would like to explain that...

There are several reasons for...

The reason why...is that...

As for the..., I think...is better.

I believe that...is a good choice for...

结尾部分，考生需要进行礼貌性回复，表达自己期待保持联系或表示感谢，下面是常见表达：

Thank you very much!

Look forward to your early reply.

Look forward to hearing from you soon.

（二）典型例题及详解

1.

You have received this email from the receptionist of a shoe store.

> From: Miss. Jones
>
> We hope you enjoyed your recent visit to our shop. We are writing to inform you that we've found your wallet in the corner of the bench in our store. Hope it hasn't caused you too much trouble. Please come by to collect your wallet at your earliest convenience.
>
> Miss Jones（Receptionist）

Write an email to Miss Jones:

• give the receptionist your opinion of the shop

• describe how losing your wallet has affected you

• say when you can come and collect your wallet?

Write at least 50 words.

观察上面的内容可以发现，这是鞋店接待员发送给顾客的一封邮件，邮件中提到接待员在店内发现了收件人的钱包，通知收件人尽快将钱包取回。

邮件下方是三点任务要求，在回复的邮件中，考生需要根据三点要求的内容分别进行陈述说明，即向接待员表达你对商店的看法、描述丢失钱包对你的影响以及询问什么时候可以来取钱包。

下面是一则范文：

Dear Miss Jones,

Thank you for informing me about my lost wallet. I guess I must have dropped it while I was trying shoes.

这封邮件的内容属于通知，但发件人和收件人并非朋友关系，因此在称呼和邮件语言表达上较正式、礼貌。称呼使用的Dear+Miss+姓氏，表达了对对方的尊敬。开头段首先表达了对收件人的感激之情。然后对丢失钱包的原因进行了猜测 "I guess I must have dropped it while I was trying shoes"。

I did enjoy visiting your shop, as I ended up buying several pairs of sneakers for my son and me. As always, the styles and prices of your shoes are hard to beat, which is why I'm a regular customer.

主体部分第一段中，作者对第一个要点进行了回复。作者表示很愿意逛鞋店，对鞋的价格和款式进行了正面回复，同时表示自己是鞋店的老客户。

Losing my wallet hasn't caused me too much trouble, though I was really worried because there are my credit cards, ID card and driver's license. In fact, I was just about to cancel my credit cards, but thankfully I don't have to anymore.

主体部分第二段中，作者对第二个要点进行了回复。详细说明了丢失钱包对自己的影响以及自己可能采取的措施。

If it's okay with you, I'd like to go collect my wallet tomorrow morning. According to your website, your shop opens at 10 a.m., so I'll stop by then.

主体部分的最后一段，作者对题目中的最后一点要求进行了说明。说明了可以去取钱包的具体时间。

Once again, thank you so much for finding my wallet and letting me know!

Yours sincerely,

Vincent

最后结尾部分，作者对接待员找到他的钱包并通知他再次表示感谢。祝福语部分，"Yours sincerely" 的使用表达出发件人对接待员的礼貌和尊敬。这篇邮件的字数为153个单词，符合题目中的字数要求，同时对题目中的三个要点都进行了回复。

下面是完整的范文：

Dear Miss Jones,

Thank you for informing me about my lost wallet. I guess I must have dropped it while I was trying shoes.

I did enjoy visiting your shop, as I ended up buying several pairs of sneakers for my son and me. As always, the styles and prices of your shoes are hard to beat, which is why I'm a regular customer.

Losing my wallet hasn't caused me too much trouble, though I was really worried because there are my credit cards, ID card and driver's license. In fact, I was just about to cancel my credit cards, but thankfully I don't have to anymore.

If it's okay with you, I'd like to go collect my wallet tomorrow morning. According to your website, your shop opens at 10 a.m., so I'll stop by then.

Once again, thank you so much for finding my wallet and letting me know!

Yours sincerely,

Vincent

范文翻译：

亲爱的琼斯小姐：

谢谢你告诉我关于钱包丢了的事。我想我一定是在试鞋的时候把它掉了。

我很喜欢逛你们的商店，因为我最后为我和我儿子买了几双运动鞋。你们鞋子的款式和价格一直都很有竞争力，这也是为什么我是你们的常客。

虽然丢了钱包并没有给我带来太多的麻烦，但我真的很担心，因为里面有我的信用卡、身份证和驾照。事实上，我正准备挂失我的信用卡，但谢天谢地，我不必这样做了。

如果可以的话，我想明天早上去取钱包。根据你们网站上提供的信息，你们的店上午十点开门，所以我会在上午十点去你们店里。

再次感谢你找到我的钱包并告诉我！

谨启，
文森特

➢ 重点词汇及短语

1. lost [lɒst] *adj.* 失去的；丢失的

2. wallet ['wɒlɪt] *n.* 钱包，皮夹子

3. guess [ges] *vt.* 猜测；估计

4. drop [drɒp] *vt.* 落下，掉下，使落下

5. sneaker ['sniːkə（r）] *n.* 橡皮底运动布鞋

6. cancel ['kænsl] *vt.* 取消，终止

7. thankfully ['θæŋkfəli] *adv.* 幸亏；高兴地，感激地

8. anymore ['enɪmɔː] *adv.* （不）再；目前

9. collect [kə'lekt] *vt.* 领取；收走

10. regular customer 老主顾

11. credit card 信用卡

➤ 重点句型及例句

1. inform sb. about sth. 告诉某人某事

　　例：Please inform us about any changes of address.

　　　　地址若有变动请通知我们。

2. end up doing sth. 以……而告终

　　例：And whatever they end up doing, they will be teaching themselves a great deal.

　　　　无论他们最终做什么，都会受益匪浅。

2.

　　You have received this email from the manager of a restaurant where you have made a group booking.

Dear Sir,

I'm writing about your booking at 1 p.m. on Friday. Can you tell me the number of people in your group, please? Also, the menu is on the restaurant website—it will help us if you can order food for your group in advance. If there is anything else you need, please let me know.

Gemma Chen

　　Write an email to Gemma Chen:

- say how many people are coming
- explain why you can't order food in advance
- tell Gemma where your group wants to sit.

　　Write at least 50 words.

　　观察上面的邮件可以发现，这是餐厅经理发送给顾客的一封邮件，邮件的内容是关于餐厅预订的情况。餐厅经理想要询问就餐的人数以及是否能根据网站上提供的菜单提前预订食物。

　　邮件下方是三点任务要求，考生需要对三个任务点分别进行陈述，即说明有多少人来就餐、解释为什么不能提前在网上订餐以及希望坐在餐厅的什么位置就餐。

下面是一则范文：

Dear Ms. Chen,

Very glad to receive your email about the group booking!

这封邮件是顾客发送给餐厅经理的，两人之间不是特别熟悉，称呼中Dear一词属于正式用语，表达了对对方的尊敬。同时，根据收件人姓名，可判断出对方是女性，因为不知道女士是否已婚，因此用Miss或Mrs.称呼女士是不合适的，Ms.的使用可以避免这种错误，同时表达出对对方的尊重。开头寒暄语中表达了对收到邮件的感激之情。

We have to meet our important clients this Friday, so the lunch is very important. Our colleague recommended your restaurant, as the food in your restaurant is excellent. There will be six employees from our company and five clients attending the meeting, so in total there will be eleven people going to your restaurant.

邮件主体部分第一段中，作者对写作要求中的第一个要点进行了回复，即有多少人来就餐。在这一段中，作者不仅说明了有多少人就餐，还对就餐的原因和选择这家餐厅的原因进行了说明。

I know there is a menu on your restaurant's website. However, we are not familiar with the appetites of our clients, so it is best for them to order at the restaurant themselves.

邮件主体部分第二段是对写作要求中第二个要点的回复，作者详细说明了不能在网上提前订餐的原因："we are not familiar with the appetites of our clients, so it is best for them to order at the restaurant themselves."这个原因合情合理，餐厅也可以理解。

On the other hand, we know that your restaurant is known for the good dining environment, and it is important for us to have an elegant dining environment, so could you please arrange a separate room with a window looking into the garden for us?

邮件主体部分第三段中，作者对第三个任务点进行了说明，即希望坐在餐厅的什么位置就餐。在这里作者对自己的请求进行了陈述，态度较委婉，疑问句的使用也可以更好地表达作者的恳求之情。

Thanks in advance!

Best wishes!

Carrier

最后部分是祝福语和发件人姓名，表达了对对方回复的期待。这篇邮件的字数为152个单词，符合题目中的字数要求。第一部分的题目中，在时间允许的情况下，考生应该多组织语言，在没有严重语法错误的情况下，更多的单词数有助于整体分数的提高。

完整的范文如下：

Dear Ms. Chen,

Very glad to receive your email about the group booking!

We have to meet our important clients this Friday, so the lunch is very important. Our colleague recommended your restaurant, as the food in your restaurant is excellent. There will be six employees from our company and five clients attending the meeting, so in total there will be eleven people going to your restaurant.

I know there is a menu on your restaurant's website. However, we are not familiar with the appetites of our clients, so it is best for them to order at the restaurant themselves.

On the other hand, we know that your restaurant is known for the good dining environment, and it is important for us to have an elegant dining environment, so could you please arrange a separate room with a window looking into the garden for us?

Thanks in advance!

Best wishes!
Carrier

范文翻译：

亲爱的陈女士：

很高兴收到你关于团体预订的邮件！

这个星期五我们要见一个重要的客户，所以午餐很重要。我们的同事推荐了贵餐厅，因为贵餐厅的食物非常棒。我们公司将有6名员工和5名客户参加聚餐，总共有11人去贵餐厅。

我知道贵餐厅网站上有菜单，但是我们不太了解客户的胃口，所以最好还是让他们自己去餐厅点。

另一方面，我们知道贵餐厅以良好的用餐环境而闻名，有一个良好的就餐环境对我们来说很重要，您能否为我们安排一间独立的有窗户可以看到花园的房间？

提前感谢您！

祝好！
卡里尔

➢重点词汇及短语

---

1. colleague [ˈkɒliːg] *n.* 同事

2. recommend [rekəˈmend] *vt.* 推荐；举荐；介绍

3. menu [ˈmenjuː] *n.* 菜单

4. appetite [ˈæpɪtaɪt] *n.* 食欲；胃口

5. order [ˈɔːdə（r）] *vt.* 点（酒菜等）

6. elegant [ˈelɪgənt] *adj.* 优美的；典雅的；简洁的

7. arrange [əˈreɪndʒ] *vt.* 安排；筹备

8. separate [ˈsepəreɪt] *adj.* 单独的；独立的

9. group booking 团体预订

10. in total 总计，合计

> ➤重点句型及例句

1. be familiar with 对……熟悉

例：Residents should be familiar with these emergency information materials.

居民应熟悉这些应急信息材料。

2. it is best for sb. to do sth. 对某人来说做某事是最好的

例：It is best for us to take things easy for a week or two.

对我们来说，最好放松一两个星期。

三、其他

领思写作考试第一部分的任务类型除了提供建议和情况说明外，还有其他的一些类型，如邀请、询问服务细节等。邀请是指邀请朋友或熟悉的人跟自己一起做某事或邀请某人到自己的家中或城市进行参观；询问服务细节通常为询问更多的广告细节。虽然任务类型同前面提到的提供建议和情况说明不同，但邮件的整体结构基本相同。下面将对常用表达进行详细讲解。

（一）常用表达

1. 邀请类

在邀请类的邮件中，三点任务要求中通常会有一点明确要求考生在回复邮件中邀请某人做某事，常用的表达为：

invite ... to go to/（see）... with you

invite ... to join you somewhere

offer an invitation to your friend to visit your hometown/country

suggest a time to invite ... to your home

当看到上面的句型时，考生应该了解到在回复的邮件中需要进行邀请，同时在脑海中对邀请的内容进行组织，注意在语句的表达上体现出自己的热情，常用的表达为：

Please allow me to invite you and your ... to my place and I will prepare a fancy meal.

Do you fancy coming to my place for dinner one night? Or would you like to catch a movie instead? It's up to you.

I'm wondering if you'd like to go...with me.

Can't wait to see you.

I am looking forward to your arrival.

2. 询问服务细节类

　　询问服务细节类的题目多为回复广告的邮件，广告中会对服务提供方能够提供的服务内容进行描述。邮件下面的写作要求中通常会有一点要求，要求考生说明对服务提供方的哪些服务比较感兴趣以及向对方提出一个要求，这个要求通常是询问对方的服务细节及要求对方展示服务，以下是常见的表达：

explain why you are interested in...

say which...you want to...

ask for a meeting with someone...

ask for an appointment with...

request information/ ask a question about the lessons you are interested in

在邮件的开头部分，考生需要对写信事由进行说明，常用到的表达如下：

With reference to your advertisement...

I'm writing to enquire something about the advertisement...

I'm interested in the service...

（二）典型例题及详解

1.

You have seen this advertisement for a new concert.

> JAZZ CONCERT
>
> Highly acclaimed jazz concert!
>
> **CONCERT IN THE PARK**
>
> Featuring pianist Heather Kraft and The Duke Singers
>
> August 27th & 29th, 7 p.m.–10 p.m.
>
> Tickets: $ 35

Write an email to your friend Irene:

- invite Irene to go to see this concert with you

- say when you would like to go

- explain why you think Irene will enjoy this concert.

Write at least 50 words.

　　结合题目要求中的内容可以发现，考生需要给朋友写一封邮件，邀请朋友跟你一起去听一场音乐会，同时需要结合广告中提供的信息，在回复的邮件中对写作要求中提到的三点任务要求分别进行回复。三点任务要求分别为：邀请朋友跟你一起听音乐会、说明你们应该什么时候去以及为什么你认为朋友会喜欢这场音乐会。

下面是一则范文：

Hello Irene,

It's been a while since we last spoke. How are you these days?

发件人和收件人为朋友关系，因此在称呼上作者直接使用Hello+人名的形式，体现出了朋友间较亲切、随意的关系。开头段中，作者进行了简单的寒暄问候 "It's been a while since we last spoke. How are you these days?"

I'm writing because I recently came across an advertisement for a jazz concert, and I'm wondering if you'd like to go with me.

邮件主体部分第一段中，作者对写信目的进行了说明 "I'm wondering if you'd like to go with me." 同时这也是对第一个要点的回复。

According to the advertisement, there are two dates for the concert: August 27th and August 29th. For both days, the concert begins at 7p.m. and ends at 10 p.m.. Of the two days, I would suggest the 27th because that's on a weekday, so we're more likely to get front row seats. However, if you're busy on the 27th, then the 29th would be fine, too.

邮件主体部分第二段是对题目要求中第二个要点的回复，在这一部分中，作者结合广告中提供的演出时间，选择出了一个较合适的时间，并详细说明了为什么这个时间比较合适；同时作者还提到 "However, if you're busy on the 27th, then the 29th would be fine too." 对时间的选择做出了让步，使朋友可以对时间进行选择，同时表达了自己的意向。

I seriously think you would enjoy this concert since it features one of your favourite pianists, Heather Kraft. Moreover, the famous Duke Singers will be there, and everyone knows they're one of the best jazz groups in the world! Despite all this, the tickets are fairly affordable at only ＄35 per person.

邮件主体部分第三段中，作者对第三个要点进行了回复。在这一段中，作者从两个方面对自己的观点进行了论证，一方面是音乐会的表演嘉宾是朋友喜欢的钢琴家，同时演出的乐队也非常著名；另一方面，音乐会的门票价格很合理，比较实惠。根据这两方面可以推断出朋友会喜欢这场音乐会。

Anyway, let me know if you'd like to go.

Best wishes,

Maria

　　最后部分是结束祝福语和发件人姓名。这篇邮件的字数为167个单词，符合题目中的字数要求。同时邮件内容对题目中的三个要点分别进行了回复，并且很好地结合了原始邮件中的内容，可以算作一篇优秀的作文。

　　下面是完整的范文：

参考答案

Hello Irene,

It's been a while since we last spoke. How are you these days?

I'm writing because I recently came across an advertisement for a jazz concert, and I'm wondering if you'd like to go with me.

According to the advertisement, there are two dates for the concert: August 27th and August 29th. For both days, the concert begins at 7 p.m. and ends at 10 p.m.. Of the two days, I would suggest the 27th because that's on a weekday, so we're more likely to get front row seats. However, if you're busy on the 27th, then the 29th would be fine, too.

I seriously think you would enjoy this concert since it features one of your favourite pianists, Heather Kraft. Moreover, the famous Duke Singers will be there, and everyone knows they're one of the best jazz groups in the world! Despite all this, the tickets are fairly affordable at only $35 per person.

Anyway, let me know if you'd like to go.

Best wishes,
Maria

范文翻译：

你好艾琳：

我们有一段时间没联系了。你最近好吗？

我写信是因为我最近看到了一个爵士音乐会的广告，我想知道你是否愿意和我一起去。

根据广告内容，两场音乐会的日期分别是8月27日和8月29日。这两天的音乐会都是晚上7点开始，10点结束。在这两天中，我建议选27号那天，因为那天是工作日，所以我们更有可能买到前排的座位。但是，如果27号你很忙，那么29号也可以。

我真的认为你会喜欢这场音乐会，因为它有你最喜欢的钢琴家之一——希瑟·克拉夫特。此外，著名的杜克合唱团也会到场，大家都知道他们是世界上最好的爵士乐队之一！除此之外，门票是相当实惠的，每人只需35美元。

不管怎样，如果你想去，告诉我一声。

祝好，
玛丽亚

➤ 重点词汇及短语

1. advertisement [əd'vɜːtɪsmənt] *n.* 广告；启事

2. jazz [dʒæz] *n.* 爵士乐

3. concert ['kɒnsət] *n.* 音乐会

4. weekday ['wiːkdeɪ] *n.* 工作日

5. row [rəʊ] *n.* （剧院、电影院等的）一排座位

6. seriously ['sɪəriəsli] *adv.* 严重地；严肃地；认真地

7. feature ['fiːtʃə（r）] *vt.* 以……为特色；由……主演

8. pianist ['pɪənɪst] *n.* 钢琴弹奏者；钢琴家

9. despite [dɪ'spaɪt] *prep.* 即使；尽管

10. fairly ['feəli] *adv.* 一定地；相当地

11. affordable [ə'fɔːdəbl] *adv.* 价格合理的；买得起的

➤重点句型及例句

1. be wondering 想知道……

例：I was just wondering if you could help me.

不知你是否能帮助我。

2. be more likely to do 更有可能……

例：When people are bored, they're more likely to feel less meaning in their lives.

当人们感到无聊时，他们更有可能觉得生活的意义愈发少了。

2.

You have seen this advertisement for winter classes on a noticeboard.

Are you looking for a new challenge? Places are still available on the winter courses listed below, all starting in November:

Pottery

Painting

Creative writing

Dance

Singing

If you're interested, email Miss Jones (Director of Studies) at binghamptoncollege. com

---

Write an email to Miss Jones:

• say which course you want to have

• explain why you are interested in the course

• ask a question about the course you're interested in.

Write at least 50 words.

　　观察上面的邮件可以发现，这是一则广告，广告中显示的是冬季班的课程情况，上面显示了可报名的课程名称以及报名联系人的信息。

　　广告下方为邮件写作的三点任务要求，考生需要在回复的邮件中说明自己想要学习的课程，同时需要说明自己对课程感兴趣的原因，最后针对自己感兴趣的课程，考生还需要提出相关问题。

　　下面是一则范文：

Dear Miss Jones,

I am excited to learn that winter classes in creative writing are being offered because I've always been very passionate about writing.

邮件开始部分，通过题目开头部分的介绍可知，虽然题目内容属于通用类，但作者和收件人并不熟悉，所以称呼部分使用的是Dear+Miss+姓氏的结构，表现出对收件人的尊敬。开头段中，作者表达了对课程开课的兴奋，同时说明了自己兴奋的原因，即"I've always been very passionate about writing."

According to the advertisement, I could choose between pottery, painting, creative writing, dance, and singing classes. Out of these five classes, I'm most interested in creative writing. I've always been an avid reader and writer, so I think the creative writing class would appeal to my own interests most.

主体部分第一段中，作者对第一个要点进行了回复。在这里作者对自己要选择的课程的名称及选择的原因进行了概括说明，即 "Out of these five classes, I'm most interested in creative writing. I've always been an avid reader and writer, so I think the creative writing class would appeal to my own interests most."

I'm interested in the course mainly because I am seeking to improve my own writing. Specifically, I've written some short fiction stories and I'd like to get some feedback and constructive criticism. Moreover, I am looking forward to learning some useful descriptive writing techniques from the course and implementing them in my own writing.

主体部分第二段中，作者对第二个要点进行了回复。虽然第一段中也有对选择原因的说明，但并不详细，这一段中，作者对原因进行了详细的说明。

Finally, I would appreciate some information about the overall structure and organization of the course. I'm curious about whether it would be primarily lecture-based or workshop-based. Also, could you please tell me how many students are usually in the creative writing class?

主体部分第三段是对最后一个要点的回复，在这一段中，作者主要提出了两个问题，分别是课程结构和学生人数，即"I'm curious about whether it would be primarily lecture-based or workshop-based." 以及 "could you please tell me how many students are usually in the creative writing class?"

Thank you for your time.

Best regards,

Alice

最后部分是祝福语和发件人姓名，作者在此表达了感谢。这篇邮件的字数为178个单词，符合题目中的字数要求。作者对三个要点做了充分说明，同时对内容进行了合理延展，整篇文章思路清晰，逻辑严谨。

下面是完整的范文：

Dear Miss Jones,

I am excited to learn that winter classes in creative writing are being offered because I've always been very passionate about writing.

According to the advertisement, I could choose between pottery, painting, creative writing, dance, and singing classes. Out of these five classes, I'm most interested in creative writing. I've always been an avid reader and writer, so I think the creative writing class would appeal to my own interests most.

I'm interested in the course mainly because I am seeking to improve my own writing. Specifically, I've written some short fiction stories and I'd like to get some feedback and constructive criticism. Moreover, I am looking forward to learning some useful descriptive writing techniques from the course and implementing them in my own writing.

Finally, I would appreciate some information about the overall structure and organization of the course. I'm curious about whether it would be primarily lecture-based or workshop-based. Also, could you please tell me how many students are usually in the creative writing class?

Thank you for your time.

Best regards,
Alice

范文翻译：

亲爱的琼斯小姐，

得知这里开设了创意写作的冬季课程我真的很兴奋，因为我一直对写作充满热情。

根据广告，我可以选择陶艺、绘画、创意写作、舞蹈和歌唱课程。在这五门课中，我最感兴趣的是创意写作。我一直是一个热爱阅读和写作的人，所以我认为创意写作课最符合我自己的兴趣。

我对这门课感兴趣主要是因为我想提高自己的写作水平。具体来说，我写了一些短篇小说故事，我希望得到一些反馈和建设性的批评。此外，我希望从这门课中学到一些有用的描述性写作技巧，并将其运用到自己的写作中。

最后，我想了解一下关于课程的总体结构和安排的一些信息。我很好奇该课程主要是讲座型还是工作坊型。另外，你能告诉我创意写作课通常有多少学生吗？

谢谢你的宝贵时间。

祝好，

爱丽丝

➤ 重点词汇及短语

1. excited [ɪkˈsaɪtɪd] *adj.* 激动的；兴奋的

2. creative [kriˈeɪtɪv] *adj.* 创造（性）的；创作的

3. passionate [ˈpæʃənət] *adj.* 热烈的；激昂的

4. pottery [ˈpɒtəri] *n.* 陶器（尤指手工制的）

5. avid [ˈævɪd] *adj.* 热衷的；酷爱的

6. improve [ɪmˈpruːv] *vt.* 改进；改善

7. specifically [spəˈsɪfɪkli] *adv.* 具体来说；确切地说

8. fiction [ˈfɪkʃn] *n.* 小说；虚构的故事

9. feedback [ˈfiːdbæk] *n.* 反馈的意见（或信息）

10. constructive [kənˈstrʌktɪv] *adj.* 建设性的；有助益的；积极的

11. criticism [ˈkrɪtɪsɪzəm] *n.* 批判；指责；（书籍或音乐等）评论

12. descriptive [dɪˈskrɪptɪv] *adj.* 描写的；叙述的；说明的

13. technique [tekˈniːk] *n.* 技术；技能

14. implement [ˈɪmplɪmənt] *vt.* 使生效；贯彻；执行；实施

15. appreciate [əˈpriːʃieɪt] *vt.* 欣赏；赏识；重视

16. overall [ˌəʊvərˈɔːl] *adj.* 全面的；综合的；总体的

17. organization [ˌɔːgənaɪˈzeɪʃn] *n.* 组织（工作）；安排，编排；条理

18. curious [ˈkjʊəriəs] *adj.* 求知欲强的；好奇的

19. primarily [praɪˈmerəli] *adv.* 主要地；根本地

➤ 重点句型及例句

1. be offered... 被提供……

例：Students would be offered on-the-job training leading to the certification of their skill in a particular field.

学生将获得在职培训，他们也将因此得到在某一领域的技术合格证。

2. be passionate about... 对……很热情

例：We all need to be passionate about something in life, and we must follow our heart.

我们都需要对生活中的某件事充满激情，我们必须追随自己的内心。

3. be most interested in... 对……尤其感兴趣

例：Other researchers would be most interested in the section of procedures.

其他的研究人员对过程部分尤为感兴趣。

4. appeal to sth. 对……有吸引力

例：It's a movie that will appeal to the young.

这是一部对年轻人有吸引力的电影。

5. seek to do sth. 试图做；设法做某事

例：Do not seek to do the best，just to do better!

不求做得最好，只求做得更好！

6. look forward to doing sth. 盼望着做某事；期盼做某事

例：We also look forward to doing more deals with you.

我们也期待着与您进行更多的交易。

Day 4　实战篇

1.

You have received this email from your friend Leonard.

From: Leonard

Hello! I'm spending the holiday in your city next week. I'm considering staying closer to the city centre, but I'm not entirely sure. Have you got any ideas about what I could do during my stay? We should meet up if you're free.

Leonard

Write an email to your friend Leonard:

• say where you think your friend should stay

• recommend some things for your friend to do

• suggest a time when you can meet your friend

Write at least 50 words.

2.

A trip with your class

Last week you went on a trip with some students from your class.

Write an email to your friend, Joseph. In your email:

• say where you went

• say what you did

• say why you enjoyed the trip.

Write at least 50 words.

3.

You have received this email from the manager of a restaurant

From: Mr. Richard

We hope you and your friends enjoyed your recent visit to our restaurant. After you left, we found a scarf and a pair of gloves under the table where you were sitting. Do these things belong to you, or your friends?

Mr. Richard（Manager）

Write an email to Mr. Richard:

- give the manager your opinion of the restaurant
- explain who the scarf and gloves belong to
- say when you can come and collect the items

Write at least 50 words.

4.

You have received this email from a college friend.

You know I told you I wanted to get fit. Well, I've just joined in the same sports centre as you did. I wonder if you could recommend some good classes to attend. And could you tell me the best time to go? I don't want to go when it's too busy. It would be great if we could meet up sometime to attend a class together or maybe have a coffee?

Email me back when you get time.

William

Write an email to William:

- recommend some classes at the sports centre
- explain the best time periods to visit the sports centre
- invite William to meet you at the sports centre café

Write at least 50 words.

Part 2　长文本

Day 5　基础篇——题型介绍

一、题型简介

在领思写作考试的第二部分中，考生需要读一段描述某场景的文字，然后根据场景中的信息和三个要点写一篇不少于180个单词的小短文、评论、信件、意见、邮件或者帖子。该部分的答题时间为30分钟。如何组织、扩展回答是考生必须具备的基本技能。

二、考试界面

领思写作考试两个部分的界面是可以相互切换的，第二部分的界面跟第一部分的基本相同。不同之处在于页面左半部分显示的试题内容为Part 2，同时第二部分建议的答题时间是30分钟。考生需要根据题目中提供的文字内容及三个要点，以及题目中要求的体裁来完成大作文的写作。如果答完第二部分之后还有剩余时间，考生可以点击右下角的箭头返回第一部分进行作答或修改。

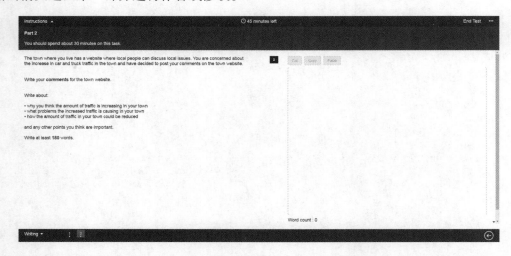

三、答题步骤

领思通用写作考试第二部分为长文本写作，涉及的体裁包括小短文、评论、信件、意见、邮件或者帖子，在写作的过程中考生可以按照下面的步骤进行：

（一）阅读题目要求，明确体裁

答题前考生需要仔细阅读屏幕左侧的题目要求及背景内容，题目中会规定具体的写作体裁。考生在写作的过程中需要根据规定体裁的固定格式来写作，避免造成体裁或格式错误。

（二）仔细阅读要点内容，注意整体逻辑性

在对要点内容进行构思的过程中，考生需要注意内容的逻辑性。每个要点需要分别进行回复，同时还需要注意保持文章整体内容的逻辑性。

（三）确定文章结构及主体段落

在正式书写之前，需要确定好文章的整体结构。按照小短文、评论、信件、意见、邮件或者帖子的固定格式确定开头段、主体段和结尾段需要表达的内容，以及主体段中每个段落的陈述要点。

（四）对文章进行整体输出

确定了整体结构和主体段的内容之后，考生需要将自己的思路在电脑上进行输出。输出的过程中考生需要控制好进度。考生需要在30分钟的时间内完成不少于180个单词的文字表达，这需要考生把握好时间，同时还需要注意单词拼写及句子表达等。

（五）提交前检查

在提交答案之前，请花3~5分钟检查完成的文章。检查的内容包括文章体裁是否正确、思路是否清晰、语气是否符合题目要求、单词拼写和标点的使用是否正确、语法结构和字词的使用是否正确、合理等。

四、写作结构

写作考试第二部分的体裁主要包括小短文、评论、信件、意见、邮件或者帖子，这几种体裁的典型文章结构如下所示：

开头段 Introduction	对文章的写作目的进行说明，或对题目内容进行改写
主体段1 Body Paragraph 1	回应第一个要点（给出细节、理由或者例子）
主体段2 Body Paragraph 2	回应第二个要点（给出细节、理由或者例子）
主体段3 Body Paragraph 3	回应第三个要点（给出细节、理由或者例子）

第二部分的文章写作应该包括一个简短的开头段和三个主体段。开头段需要对文章的写作目的进行一个总的说明，或者对下文中要进行说明的三个要点进行概括总结。

通常，每个主体段需要回应一个要点。另外，考生需要记住，每个主体段中应该包含一个主题句，整个段落围绕主题句展开说明，可以通过细节描写、理由说明或举例来展开内容。第二部分写作题目中，作者可以将回应第三个要点的第三个主体段作为结尾段。此外，通用考试中的写作主题多是与生活相关的话题，语域特点应该介于中性文体与非正式文体之间，且偏向于非正式文体，因此考生在词汇和语言表述上可多倾向于非正式表达，同时注意表达的语气既要得体又要有礼貌。

（一）开头部分

在第二部分写作的开头（Introduction）中，考生可以简单地用一句话清楚地复述题目，也可以对观点进行总结概括，展示自己的写作目的和立场。

在开头部分的写作中，考生需要注意以下两点：

➢ 在开头段直接表明自己的写作目的，如对某件事情的评论、看法或意见，写信的理由，或者表明要陈述的事由等。

➢ 开头段必须陈述题目的主题：对于题目中要求表达的观点和需要陈述的问题，开头段需要明确说明，不能陈述与题目主题无关的内容。

在第二部分的写作题目中，不同的开头段表达方式可用于不同的体裁中，下面将进行举例说明：

题目（1）

The new school year

Your school magazine is going to publish a special edition to welcome students back to school for the new school year. You have been asked to write an article about the importance of setting study goals, the type of goals a student should set, and where students can find the support they need to achieve their goals.

In your article you should write:

• the importance of setting study goals

• what type of goals students should set

• where students can find the support they need to achieve their goals

and any other points you think are important.

Write at least 180 words.

开头段表达：

I am writing this article to express my opinion on what learning goals students should set for the new school year and the importance of setting learning goals.

题目（2）

Banning the use of mobile phones

Your town council is thinking about banning the use of mobile phones on public transport and in shops and restaurants.

Write a letter to the town council.

You should write:

· what is your opinion about banning the use of mobile phones

· tell the reasons why you think it is or is not a good idea

· what are the measures to take to ban the use of mobile phones in the public

and any other points you think are important.

Write at least 180 words.

开头段表达：

I am writing this letter to express my opinion on whether to ban mobile phones in public places, why should we do so, and the specific measures to ban mobile phones.

> 观察上面两个范例的开头段表达可以发现，开头段仅包含一句话，这句话是对写作要求中的内容进行的相应改写，从而我们可以了解到，通过对写作要点进行改写可以很好地概括文章的写作目的。

题目（3）

You have seen this notice on your college website.

> **Write us a review of a website that you have used for studying!**
> Tell us about a website that you have used for studying. What is good about it? Could it be improved? Who would you recommend the website to?

Write a review of a website that you have used for studying.

Write about:

· why you like the website

· what could make the website better

· who you would recommend the website to

and any other points which you think are important.

Write at least 180 words.

开头段表达：

In this review, I will talk about a useful website I have used for my studies. I will explain its merits, as well as those aspects in which it should be improved and I will recommend this website to beginners in the language learning and those who have to do some translation tasks.

题目（4）

Your local council is inviting comments on its website from locals about a proposal to build a theme park in your town to attract tourists. You are concerned that a theme park will destroy the image of your town and decide to leave a comment on the website.

Write your comments on the town website.

Write about:

• how a theme park is inappropriate for a historic town

• why you think increased tourism will destroy your town

• an alternative way to improve your town

and any other points you think are important.

Write at least 180 words.

开头段表达：

I was very concerned to read that the council is planning to build a theme park in the middle of our historic town. How can anyone think it is a good idea to construct an inappropriate modern scenery in the middle of a place of beautiful and impressive architecture?

> 上面两个范例的开头段直接对题目要求中的内容进行了概括性回复，同时加入了描述性和评论性的表达，这样能更好地吸引读者，同时也会让读者在文章开头就了解到作者的观点和写作意图。

（二）主体部分

在写作考试第二部分的试题中，题目要求中会列出三个问题，考生回答这三个问题的过程也是对文章内容进行思索的过程，考生可以根据线索支撑起整篇文章的脉络走向，当问题中出现what、why或how时，考生可以根据问题依次作答，同时注意保持文章整体条理清晰、衔接自然。

在对主体部分进行作答时，应该注意以下几个方面：

1. 每个段落分别对应题目中的一个问题；

2. 每个主体段落中都应该包含一个主题句，主题句应该陈述并回应写作要求中提到的问题；

3. 明确写作要求中的关键词，做出清晰回复。

如何进行观点拓展

在第二部分的题目中，考生需要在30分钟内完成不少于180个单词的作文写作，这对考生的思维拓展能力和打字速度都是一种考验。考生平时需要多加练习，在提高打字速度的同时还需要掌握相应的写作方法，对观点进行拓展是每个考生都应该具备的能力，只有这样才能让写作的内容更充实，文章更有说服力。

对观点进行充分拓展和支撑，这一点对文章的整体表达和字数控制来说都是非常重要的。这样，文章的观点将更具说服力。拓展观点的方法有很多种，下面将对几种主要的方法进行说明：

1. 添加细节

恰当使用连接词来添加细节，对观点进行扩展。根据不同的连接作用，可以使用不同的连接词和连接短语，下面为几类主要的连接词和短语：

顺序先后	first of all, firstly, to begin with, the first reason is that, to start with, primarily, first and foremost, secondly, the second reason is that, another reason is that, finally, as a final point, to conclude with, thirdly, lastly, finally, the final reason is that
时间先后	now, at present, recently, after, afterwards, after that, after a while, in a few days, at first, later, next, finally, immediately, soon, suddenly, all of a sudden, at that moment, as soon as, the moment, from now on, from then on, at the same time, meanwhile, till, not...until, before, after, when, while, as, during
递进	also, in addition, moreover, furthermore, in fact, actually, not to mention（this）, what's more
转折	but, however, in contrast, while, whereas, though, although, otherwise, except（for）, instead, nevertheless, nonetheless, on the contrary
因果	as a result, consequently, for this reason, therefore, because, because of, since, now that, as, thanks to..., due to..., so...that, such...that
解释说明	now, in addition, for example, for instance, in this case, moreover, furthermore, in fact, actually
条件	as（so）long as, on condition that, if, unless

让步	even if, even though, whether... or..., whoever, whatever, whichever, wherever, whenever, no matter how（who, what, which, where, when, whom）, despite, in spite of
举例	for example, for instance, such as..., take...for example
比较	be similar to, similarly, the same as, in contrast, compared with（to）..., just like, just as
目的	for this reason, for this purpose, so that, in order to , so as to
概括归纳	in a word, in short, in brief, on the whole, generally speaking, in my opinion, as far as I know, as we all know, as has been stated, as I have shown, finally, at last, in summary, in conclusion
选择	either...or..., neither...nor, or, as well as..., both...and....

2. 提供理由

对理由进行说明也是拓展回答的一种方法，既能对选择和决定的原因进行说明，也能使文章结构更严谨。常用的句子结构包括以下两种：

➡原因状语从句

由 because（因为），as（由于），since（既然），now（that）（既然），when（既然），seeing（that）（由于、鉴于），considering（that）（考虑到），for（因为），given（that）（考虑到）等引导的原因状语从句都可以对原因进行说明，在第二部分的写作中可以根据要表达的意思进行适当添加。

➡其他能够表达因果关系的句式

在英语中，有些句式和固定表达可以起到解释的作用，这些句式也可以用于观点拓展，常见的句式包括：

That's why...

Therefore, ...

As a result, ...

This is because...

Thanks to...

On account of...

Due to...

3. 提供对比

英语表达中，对比可以将事物的特征更清晰地表达出来，同时作者的观点也能得到更好的呈现。在观点拓展中，常用的对比方法包括以下几种：

→比较级的使用

比较级是英语中最直接表达对比的方法，在句子中使用比较级时需要注意两个事物之间的比较关系，同时注意不同形容词和副词的比较级变化形式和使用规则。

→具有表达和引导对比关系的词及词组

英语中有些词和词组可以表达对比的关系，这些词通常含有转折关系。在观点拓展中，这些词的使用可以更好地突出作者的观点，常见的词汇如下：

however：意为"然而；不管怎样"，表示转折的关系，常用于引导两个句子，表示比较的含义；

but：意为"但是，然而"，常用于引导句子内部的对比；

rather than：意为"而不是"，可以展示一个句子内的对比或两个句子的对比关系；

instead：意为"反而；却"，同 rather than 用法类似，可以展示一个句子内的对比或两个句子的对比关系。

→具有对比关系的固定词组

英语中有些词组的使用在对两方面的情况进行说明的同时，可以形成对比关系，常见的表达有：

On one hand...On the other hand...：一方面……另一方面……

Neither...nor...：既不……也不……

4. 举例说明

提供具体的例子是拓展观点的另一种方法。具体的例子可以更具体地说明观点，增强说服力，同时使文章结构更紧凑。常用结构如下：

For example, ...

For instance, ...

When I was in...

This happened last week when...

A couple years ago, I...

5. 通过描述时间以及与过去或未来进行比较

对过去或未来的事情进行描述时，可以跟现在的情况进行对比，从而对观点进行扩展。

常用的时间连接词有 recently, in recent years, currently, used to, in the past, compared to the past, many years ago, in the future, later on。

6. 对之前的话进行总结概括

在对一件事情进行说明之后或在段落结尾，可以通过重述的方式对前面说过的话进行解释或强调。常用的表达有：

In other words, ...

This means that...

In all, .../ To all, ...

In short, ...

Broadly speaking,

In brief, .../ To be brief, .../ Briefly, ...

In a few words, ...

In sum, ...

Anyway, .../ Anyhow, ...

Altogether, .../ All in all, ...

To sum up, ...

As a result, .../ In one word, ...

At any rate, ...

First and last, ...

五、常见表达问题

在领思写作考试第二部分的长文本写作中，语法点是一个评分维度，考生在平时的练习中需要注意语法知识点的积累。经常出现的表达问题包括主谓不一致、句子完整性错误和各种表达错误。这里将对经常出现的问题进行详细说明，考生可进行积累。

(一) 主谓不一致

英文写作中，在复杂结构和长主语的干扰下，句子结构会变得复杂，构成主语的单词变多，从而在写谓语的时候容易忽视主语，导致主谓不一致。

所谓主谓一致就是谓语动词在人称和数上与主语保持一致。人称指的是做句子主语的名词和代词，数指的是谓语动词的单复数变化。

主谓一致原则主要包括三方面，分别是：语法一致原则、意义一致原则和就近一致原则。

1. 语法一致

语法一致原则是指，主语和谓语在语法形式上取得一致，即主语是单数形式，谓语也采取单数形式；主语是复数形式，谓语也采取复数形式。

A grammar book helps you learn something about the rules of a language. 语法书

帮助你学习语言的规则。

（主语是单数形式，谓语也采取单数形式）

Grammar books help you learn something about the rules of a language. 语法书帮助你学习语言的规则。

（主语是复数形式，谓语也采取复数形式）

主语和谓语在语法形式上取得一致的问题远不止上述那么简单，许多情况需要具体对待，下面将举例说明。

➡ 动名词、不定式以及从句做主语时，应看作单数，谓语动词用单数。

例：Smoking is bad for health. 吸烟有害健康。

To do morning exercises is useful for our health. 做早操有利于我们的健康。

What he said has been recorded. 他说的话已被录音了。

➡ 由 each, every, no, many a, either、neither 等做主语或是修饰主语时，应看作单数，谓语动词用单数。

例：Neither likes the friends of the other. 两人都不喜欢对方的朋友。

Everything around us is matter. 我们周围的所有东西都是物质。

Each man and (each) woman is asked to help. 每个人，无论男女都被请去帮忙。

➡ 表示国家、机构、事件、作品等名称的专有名词做主语时，应看作单数，谓语动词用单数。

例：*One Thousand and One Nights* tells people lots of mysterious bits of folklore. 《一千零一夜》给人们讲了许多神秘的民间传说。

China attracts many brilliant young men all over the world every year. 中国每年吸引许多来自世界各地的优秀青年。

The United Nations plays an important role in the international affairs. 联合国在国际事务中起重要作用。

➡ a series of, a kind of, the number of, a line of 等与名词构成名词短语做主语时，应看作单数，谓语动词用单数。

例：A series of high technology products has been laid out in the exhibition.
一系列高科技产品已在展览上展出。

The number of printing mistakes in some recent books often surprises people even to death.
目前一些书里的印刷错误的数量往往让人吃惊得要命。

A substantial portion of the reports is missing. 这些报告中的很大一部分不见了。

A kind of rose in the garden smells very pleasant. 这座花园里有一种玫瑰香气怡人。

➡ 由 several，both，few，many，a number of 等词修饰主语，或是它们自身做主语时，应看作复数，谓语动词用复数。

例：Both parties have their own advantages. 双方都有各自的优势。

A number of boys are singing songs. 许多男生在唱歌。

➡ 由 and 连接两个主语时，如果指同一人或物时，谓语动词用单数；指不同的人或物时，谓语动词用复数。

例：A cart and horse was seen at a distance. 远远地看到一辆马车。

The bread and the butter are on sale. 面包和黄油在打折出售。

➡ 有些短语，如 a lot of，most of，any of，half of，three fifths of，eighty percent of，some of，none of，the rest of，all of 等后接不可数名词，或是单数形式的名词做主语时，应看作单数，谓语动词用单数；但如果后接可数名词的复数形式做主语时，应看作复数，谓语动词用复数。

例：A lot of money in the shop was stolen yesterday when the electricity was suddenly cut off. 昨天突然断电时，那家商店被偷了许多钱。

The rest of the books were returned to the library. 其余的书都归还给图书馆了。

➡ 有些用来表示由两个对应部分组成一体的名词（trousers，glasses，shoes，shorts，scissors 等）做主语时，前面若有"一条""一副""一把"之类的量词，谓语动词用单数；若没有量词或量词是复数，则谓语动词用复数。

例：My glasses were broken while I played football yesterday. 昨天踢足球时我的眼镜被打碎了。

A pair of shoes is lying under the bed. 床底下有一双鞋。

Here are some new pairs of shoes. 这里有几双新鞋。

➡ 表示时间、距离、金钱等的复数名词做主语表达一个整体概念时，谓语动词常用单数，但若强调数量，谓语动词可用复数。

例：One million dollars is a lot of money. 一百万美元是一大笔钱。

2. 意义一致

意义一致即谓语动词的单复数形式由主语的意义而不是形式所决定。当主语形式为单数，但意义为复数时，谓语动词要用复数形式；但主语形式为复数，而意义却为单数时，谓语动词用单数形式。

➡ 有些名词如people，cattle，police等没有单数形式，做主语时，谓语动词只能用复数。

例：The police were sent to the spot to keep order immediately. 警察立即被派往现场维持秩序。

Cattle were allowed to graze in this area. 允许牲畜在这个地区吃草。

➡ 英语中一些单复数同形的名词做主语时，应根据其表达的意义来决定谓语动词的单复数形式。这类名词常见的有sheep，deer，fish，means，species，Chinese，Japanese，series等。

例：Every possible means has been used to prevent the air pollution. 为了防止大气污染，每一种可能的方法都试过了。

All possible means have been tried to keep animals and plants from becoming endangered. 为了阻止动植物濒临灭绝，所有可能的方法都试过了。

➡ 有些集合名词，如public, family, enemy, audience, government, group, committee, team, staff, crew等做主语时，谓语动词的数要根据其包含的意义而定。如果该名词表示一个整体，其谓语动词用单数形式；如果这些集体名词表示集合中的若干个体时，谓语动词用复数形式。

例：A team which is full of enthusiasm is more likely to win. 一支充满热情的队伍比较可能获胜。

The team are practicing hard on the playground. 队员们正在操场上刻苦地训练。

The government has taken possible actions. 政府已经采取了可能的措施。

The government are discussing the proposal. 政府正在讨论这项提案。

➡ "the +形容词或过去分词"表示一类人时，谓语动词用复数形式；"the +形容词"指一个人或表示一种抽象概念或品质时，谓语动词用单数形式。

例：The wounded were saved by the villagers at last. 最后，伤员们被村民们救起。

The wounded in the accident was a policeman. 这次事故的受伤者是一名警察。

➡ 有些以s结尾表示学科名称的词，如physics, mathematics, economics, politics等做主语时，谓语动词用单数形式。

例：Politics is a complicated subject. 政治是一门复杂的学科。

➡ such做主语时要根据其所指的内容决定谓语动词的单复数形式。

例：Such is our plan. 这就是我们的计划。

121

Such are his words. 这些就是他所说的话。

3. 就近一致

就近一致原则即谓语动词的人称和数与邻近的主语保持一致。

➡ 在 there be 结构、here 以及表示地点的介词词组位于句首引导的倒装句中，谓语动词的人称和数应与最近的一个主语保持一致。

例：There are two chairs and a desk in the office. 办公室中有两把椅子和一张桌子。

There is a pencil and several photos on the desk. 桌上有一支铅笔和几张照片。

Here is a pencil and some pens for you. 给你一支铅笔和几支钢笔。

➡ 当 either...or..., neither...nor..., not only...but also..., not...but..., or, nor 等并列连词连接两个主语时，谓语动词的人称和数应与邻近的主语保持一致。

例：Not you but I am responsible for the delay. 不是你而是我应对这次的延误负责。

Neither I nor he plays cards. 我和他都没打牌。

Not only you but (also) he is wrong. 不仅你错了，他也错了。

（二）句子完整性错误

保持一个句子的结构完整及各个成分的正确使用是考生写作文的时候需要时刻注意的问题。这里将对写作中经常出现的问题进行详细说明。

1. 句子完整性

➡ 一个简单句有两个基本成分：主语和谓语动词，两者缺一不可。

例1：In China has more than 100 million subscribers to cable television. （×）

China has more than 100 million subscribers to cable television. （√）

上面的两个例句中，第一个例句中如果加入介词 in，In China 为介词短语，句子中则缺少主语，句子结构不完整，第二个例句为正确表达。

例2：One of the many benefits of traveling overseas learning how to cope with the unexpected. （×）

One of the many benefits of traveling overseas is learning how to cope with the unexpected. （√）

上面的两个例句中，第一个例句的谓语动词使用错误，现在分词不能做句子谓语，句子缺少谓语。第二个句子中的 is 为系动词，后跟现在分词 learning 做表语，句子成分完整。

➡ 如果一个句子中包含从句，从句要保证完整。

例：Those who overweight or indulge in unhealthy diets are candidates for heart attacks.（×）

Those who are overweight or indulge in unhealthy diets are candidates for heart attacks.（√）

上面两个例句中，those后面是who引导的定语从句，修饰先行词those，who在定语从句中做主语，overweight是形容词，第一个例句缺少系动词，所以从句中的句子成分缺失，表达错误，第二个例句为正确表达。

➡ 介词后面一定要加名词、代词或者从句做宾语。

例：A marked character of cooperative learning is that personal success only springs from.（×）

A marked character of cooperative learning is that personal success only springs from group success.（√）

上面两个例句中，第一个例句的介词from后面缺少宾语，造成句意表达不完整。第二个例句为正确表达。

➡ 在大多数情况下，比较级后面一般要加than，并且清晰指明所比较的对象。

例：Divorce is more common.（×）

Divorce is more common than it was one generation ago.（√）

上面两个例句表达的是比较的含义。英语比较级的表达结构为：形容词比较级+than+比较成分。第一个例句中缺少than及后面的比较成分，句子结构不完整，第二个例句为正确表达。

2. 成分多余

下面将对各种句子成分多余的情况分别进行说明。

➡ 一个简单句通常只有一个主语，如果主语超过一个，要使用连词构成并列主语。

例：Smoking, drinking are banned in many places of work.（×）

Smoking and drinking are banned in many places of work.（√）

上面的两个例句中，主语为两个名词，两个名词中间需要用连词来连接，第一个例句中没有使用连词而是使用逗号，用法错误，第二个例句表达正确。

➡ 如果一个句子中出现多个谓语动词，要使用连词连接构成并列动词，或者在一些句子中使用关系代词构成复合句。有一些动词后面可以跟动名词做宾语或者宾语补足语。

例 1：The media distort reality, categorize things as all good or all bad. (×)

The media distort reality and categorize things as all good or all bad. (√)

例 2：It is unclear recycling can help control pollution. (×)

It is unclear whether recycling can help control pollution. (√)

例 3：It is advertising makes us buy something on a whim. (×)

It is advertising that makes us buy something on a whim. (√)

上面三组例句中，每组的第一个例句都存在缺失连词的现象，导致句子表达的意思不完整，并且句子结构存在语法错误，每组的第二个例句为正确表达。

➡ 如果一个句子中出现多个宾语，一般要使用连词连接构成并列宾语。但是也有一些动词，如 give，offer 等可以跟双宾语。

例：More people would prefer cycling, walking if conditions were right. (×)

More people would prefer cycling or walking if conditions were right. (√)

上面的例句中，prefer 后面有两个宾语，此时需要连词将两个宾语连接起来，逗号在第一个例句中的用法不正确，第二个例句中使用的连词 or 表达正确。

➡ 部分名词短语可独立做时间状语，前面不能加介词。

例：People can travel to and from duty in every day on foot or by bike. (×)

People can travel to and from duty every day on foot or by bike. (√)

上面的例句中，every day 作为时间状语，前面不需要加介词 in，类似的名词短语还有：

✦ next，last，the next，the last 加时间名词做状语前可不用介词。

例：He is going to meet my parents next week.

下周他要见我的父母。

✦ this，that，these，those 构成的时间状语前可不用介词。

例：We are going to have a new English book this year.

今年我们将有一本新英语书。

He didn't go back that night.

那晚他没有回来。

✦ 在 today，tomorrow，yesterday，the day before yesterday，the night before last，the day after tomorrow 前不用介词。

例：Who is on duty today?

今天谁值日？

He got up early yesterday.

昨天他起得早。

✦ 由one，any，each，every，some 等构成的时间状语前，可不用介词。

例：Tom gets up at six every morning.

汤姆每天早晨6点钟起床。

You can come to ask me any time you like.

你可以随时来问我。

✦ 以all 开头的时间状语（如 all the week，all day 等）之前，可以不用介词for。

例：She was busy all day yesterday.

她昨天忙了一整天。

➡ 一般来说，because 和so，although/though 和but 等连词不能够同时用在一个句子当中。

例：Although the crime rate is falling in many parts of the world，but violent crimes are constantly rampant.（×）

Although the crime rate is falling in many parts of the world，violent crimes are constantly rampant.（√ ）

第一个例句同时使用了although 和but，在这里需要注意，英语中的although/ though 为从属连词，用于引导让步状语从句；而but（但是）为并列连词，用以连接两个句子使之成为并列句。假若在同一句中既用了从属连词although/ though，又用了并列连词but，会使得句子一半像复合句，一半像并列句，从而导致句型混乱。

➡ 避免用词累赘，同义词或近义词最好不要同时出现。

例：Teamwork is indispensable，essential and crucial if you are not an experienced learner or worker.（×）

Teamwork is indispensable if you are not an experienced learner or worker.（√ ）

上面的第一个例句主句结构中的表语为三个并列的形容词，这三个形容词为近义词，均表达"关键的、必要的"意思。英文表达应简洁，避免用词累赘，相近意义的词汇使用一个即可。因此第二个例句表达正确。

（三）表达错误

1. 时态、语态使用错误

在英语表达中，时态和语态错误也是一种常见的现象，考生在平时的练习中需要多加注意。常见的错误表达如下：

➡ 情态动词后面应加动词原形。

例1：This trend may persisted for years. （×）

This trend may persist for years. （√）

例2：Clothes for travel should was lightweight and practical. （×）

Clothes for travel should be lightweight and practical. （√）

观察上面两组例句可发现，两组例句中都含有情态动词，但在每组的第一个例句中，情态动词后面的动词和系动词均为过去式，在此需要注意，情态动词后面加动词原形，因此每组中的第二个例句表达正确。

➡ 助动词be后的动词不能是原形，一定要是动词的现在分词或者过去分词形式。

例：The budget of a country should be balance each year. （×）

The budget of a country should be balanced each year. （√）

上面的例句中表达的是被动含义，因此be 动词后面应该接动词过去分词形式表示被动含义，第二个例句表达正确。

➡ 有些句子的谓语动词由助动词（或情态动词）与实义动词构成，以构成一定的语态或时态。

例：Obesity has a problem to most Americans for decades. （×）

Obesity has been a problem to most Americans for decades. （√）

上面的第二个例句中的has+been构成现在完成时，表示持续的状态，对状态进行描述；第一个例句中的has后没有实意动词，则has为实意动词，做句子谓语，has做实意动词意为"有；接受"，在句子中句意不通，所以表达错误。

➡ 动词的语态要分清主动和被动。

例1：Trade is consisted of the exchange of goods and that of services. （×）

Trade consists of the exchange of goods and that of services. （√）

在句子表达中，考生需要分清句子中的主动和被动关系。上面两个句子分别使用了主动和被动表达，根据句意此处的意思为"贸易包括商品交换和服务交换"，在英语中，consist of 通常不使用被动语态，因此第二个例句表达正确。

例2：Consumer confidence will improve, which is crucial to an economic recovery. （×）

Consumer confidence will be improved, which is crucial to an economic recovery. （√）

上面的两个例句表达的意思为"消费者的信心将得到提升"，信心和提升之间是被动关系，所以此处应该用被动表达，因此第二个例句表达正确。

➡ 被动语态中，如果谓语动词是由动介或动副短语构成且位于句尾，那么后面的介词或者副词不能省略。

例：At the nursing home, elders can be well cared. (×)

　　At the nursing home, elders can be well cared for. (√)

上面的两个例句的区别在于第二个例句中"动词+介词短语"的结构是完整的，第一个例句中缺少介词，所以第二个例句的表述是正确的。

2. 谓语动词使用错误

英语动词包括及物动词和不及物动词，这两种动词在使用上有一些区别，考生在写作的过程中需要注意两类动词的使用规则，避免出现错误。

➡ 及物动词后一定要加名词或者名词性质的成分做宾语，构成"主语+谓语动词+宾语"的基本句型；否则就是错误的。

例：I will discuss in some detail. (×)

　　I will discuss this topic in some detail. (√)

在上面两个例句中，谓语动词discuss是及物动词，后面需要加名词做宾语，第一个例句中缺少宾语，为错误表达。

➡ 不及物动词后不能直接加任何名词或名词性的词语做宾语，如果要加宾语，则要加介词；不及物动词没有被动语态。

例1：The accident was similar to the one that was happened last year. (×)

　　　The accident was similar to the one that happened last year. (√)

在上面两个例句中，happen是不及物动词，不能使用被动语态，因此第一个例句表达错误。

例2：I disagree many points made by the supporters of globalization. (×)

　　　I disagree with many points made by the supporters of globalization. (√)

在上面的例句中，谓语动词disagree是不及物动词，不能直接加宾语，如果加宾语，则需要加介词，第一个例句中的disagree后面没有加介词，为错误表达。

➡ 有些动词词组不用被动语态，常见的有depend on, rely on, survive on, arise from, stem from, belong to, consist of等。

例1：Many museums and libraries are depended entirely on donations from the public. (×)

　　　Many museums and libraries depend entirely on donations from the public. (√)

例2：A successful organization should not be consisted entirely of older people. (×)

A successful organization should not consist entirely of older people. (√)

在上面两组例句中，谓语动词均由不及物动词+介词构成，但需要注意的是有些动词词组不能使用被动语态，上面两个例句中的depend on和consist of均不能使用被动语态，因此每组中的第一个例句均为错误表达，每组中第二个例句为正确表达。

➜ 有一些及物动词后面跟宾语和宾语补足语，构成主语+谓语动词+宾语+宾语补足语的基本句型。

注意：make，have，let这三个使役动词后面跟的宾语补足语常用省略to的动词不定式。

例1：This photograph makes me to look about 60s. (×)

This photograph makes me look about 60s. (√)

例2：Whether we like it or not, our families shape our lives and make us to be what we are. (×)

Whether we like it or not, our families shape our lives and make us what we are. (√)

上面两组例句的谓语动词均为make，make属于使役动词，后面跟的宾语补足语常为省略to的动词不定式或从句，所以每组例句中的第一个例句为错误表达。

➜ 系动词后面接表语，构成主语+系动词+表语的基本句型，比如be，seem，look，get，stay，remain等。

✦ 副词不能做表语，形容词则可以。

例：Cycling is beneficially to our health. (×)

Cycling is beneficial to our health. (√)

上面两个例句为主系表结构，系动词后面加形容词构成表语，不能加副词，因此第一个例句表达错误。

✦ 系动词一般不用被动语态。

例：Most children are seemed to be better at remembering bad habits, instead of good ones. (×)

Most children seem to be better at remembering bad habits, instead of good ones. (√)

在英语表达中，系动词无被动语态，上面的第一个例句中使用的是系动词的被动语态，属于表达错误，第二个例句表达正确。

3. 词性理解错误

➜ 可数名词和不可数名词

✦ 单数可数名词前一定要加限定词，不可数名词则无此规则。

例：Computer is a machine for collecting, processing and presenting information. (×)

A computer is a machine for collecting, processing and presenting information. (√)

computer属于可数名词，在句子表达中，可数名词前需要加限定词，第一个例句中computer前面没有加任何限定词，属于表达错误。

✦ 有一些词或者短语后面要加复数可数名词（例如a few, few, a variety of, various, other, numerous, a number of, different, one of, many等）。

例：Smoking cessation is one of the likely factor that contribute to the development of obesity. (×)

Smoking cessation is one of the likely factors that contribute to the development of obesity. (√)

在英语表达中，有些短语或单词后面需要加名词的复数形式，考生在表达的过程中需要注意固定词组的使用，使用正确的单复数表达。在上面的第一个例句中，one of后面需要加可数名词的复数形式，例句中使用的是单数形式，表达错误。

✦ 有一些单词或者短语后面要加单数可数名词（例如any other, another, each, neither, either等）。

例：Many teenagers begin smoking habits due to peer pressure but not for any other reasons. (×)

Many teenagers begin smoking habits due to peer pressure but not for any other reason. (√)

上面的两个例句都出现了词组any other，表示"其他的"，any other后面的名词为可数名词的单数形式，第一个例句使用复数形式属于错误表达。

✦ 有一些词或者短语后面要加不可数名词（例如a little, little, much等）。

例：Little progresses have been made towards tackling poverty. (×)

Little progress has been made towards tackling poverty. (√)

在英语中，谓语动词的单复数形式由主语来决定，考生在写句子的过程中首先需要弄清楚主语的单复数形式。上面两个例句的主语为progress，表示"进步；进展；进程"，是不可数名词，同时前面由little来修饰。little表示"少得几乎没有；少量的"，用来修饰不可数名词时，谓语动词要用单数形式，因此第一个例句表达错误。

➜ 冠词

有一些形容词前面常加定冠词（例如only, very, same等）。

例：People with same experience should be paid same pay. （×）

People with the same experience should be paid the same pay. （√）

上面两个例句中，都用same来修饰后面的名词，same做形容词时其前面需要加定冠词，第一个例句的same前没有加定冠词，所以表达错误。

➡ 序数词和形容词最高级前要加定冠词。

例：The cigarette is most common method of smoking tobacco. （×）

The cigarette is the most common method of smoking tobacco. （√）

上面两个例句含有形容词的最高级，最高级前面需要加定冠词，第一个例句中没有加定冠词，所以表达错误。

➡ 介词

✦ 介词后不能跟句子，注意其与连词的区别。比较容易被误用为连词的介词或者介词短语有despite，in spite of，during，because of等。

例：Many smokers are unwilling to cease smoking despite they have knowledge of its ill health effects. （×）

Many smokers are unwilling to cease smoking despite their knowledge of its ill health effects. （√）

第一个例句的despite被用做连词，后面接的是完整的句子，而且despite是介词，后面不可以接句子。

✦ to在句子中可能是介词（需要加名词或者具备名词性质的内容），也可能是动词不定式符号，要根据具体情况注意区分。如，在contribute to，lead to，pay attention to，give rise to等词组中，to都是介词。

例：Public disorder can lead to damage a country's economy. （×）

Public disorder can lead to a country's economic crisis. （√）

在上面两个例句中，lead to中的to属于介词，后面直接接名词或具备名词性质的内容，第一个例句将to视为不定式符号，接了动词原形，属于错误表达。

✦ 有一些词既可以做介词也可以做连词（跟句子）（例如for，since，after，before等）。

例：Traditional buildings are desired sometimes, for the simple reason is that they are of commercial and cultural values.

Traditional buildings are desired sometimes, for the simple reason that they are of commercial and cultural values.

第一个例句中的for为连词，for后面的部分为一个完整的句子；第二个例句中，for

为介词，for后面连接的是一个名词词组 simple reason，that引导同位语从句。

六、学生习作分析

　　这一部分将对学生习作中经常出现的问题进行讲解，并给出范文，考生可以结合习作中出现的问题进行总结学习，同时可参考范文进行背诵记忆。

　　范例1

　　With the popularity of online games，more and more college students indulge in online games.

　　Write an essay about this phenomenon.

　　Write about:

* your opinions of playing online games
* the influence of online games on college students
* what college students should do to avoid the influence of online games

　　and any other points which you think are important.

　　Write at least 180 words.

　　Revision scheme

With the popularity （with是介词，后面接名词，popular是形容词，此处应该用名词） of online games, more and more college students have been drawn into a whirlpool of addiction to online games and abandoned their studies totally. I fully agree that online games have many negative effects on college students. In this essay, I will discuss the effects of online games on college students and what ~~should college students do~~ college students should do （此处为陈述句语序，情态动词should不需要提前） to avoid the influence of online games.

First, online games gravely distract students'attention from their ~~study~~studies （study做"学业"讲时应该为复数形式）, which may lead to neglecting their ~~study~~studies and then affecting their future. Second, these games endanger students'health. Sitting in front of the computer and staring at the screen for hours on end do harm to students'eyesight as well as their mental condition. Third, online games are likely to deteriorate ~~students~~ students' （此处应该为名词所有格形式） moral values. Since many online games are about violence, students may unconsciously accept the false principles and values in the games and believe that violence is a good way to settle disagreements.

As college students, we should be fully aware of the harmfulness of online games. Instead of wasting time on these games, we should make full use of our valuable college years to learn as much as we can.

Sample

> With the popularity of online games, an increasing number of college students have been ensnared in the whirpool of online game, which results in a complete abandonment of their academic pursuits. I totally agree that online games exert numerous adverse effects on college students. In this essay, I will delve into the impacts of online games on college students and how they can evade the bad influence of online games.
>
> First, online games profoundly divert students' attention away from their studies, which may lead to a neglect of their academic performances and subsequently impede their future prospects. Second, these games pose a grave threat to students' health. Prolonged hours spent sitting in front of the computer screen not jeopardize only students' eyesight but also their mental condition. Third, online games are likely to deteriorate students' moral values. Given that many online games revolve around violence, students may unconsciously accept the false principles and values in the games and believe that violence is an acceptable means of conflict resolution.
>
> As college students, it is incumbent upon us to be acutely aware of the harmfulness of online games. Instead of wasting time on these games, we should make full use of our valuable college years to acquire knowledge as much as we can.

范例2

Currently, most parks in China are free of admission for citizens, but the free opening of parks also brings some problems.

Write an essay about this phenomenon.

Write about:

- your opinions about the free opening of parks
- what negative effects it brings
- what people should do to avoid the problems

and any other points which you think are important.

Write at least 180 words.

Revision scheme

As we all know, most parks in China are ~~opened~~open（open 在此处为形容词词性，跟前面的be动词构成系表结构）to the public for free at present. The free admission to parks is implemented nationwide with the main purpose of providing the public, the rich or the poor with equal opportunities to enjoy the scenery and utilize the facilities in the parks.

Besides the benefits and conveniences, ~~there have emerged some problems~~ some problems have emerged（此处there be 结构使用不恰当）as well. Since people are allowed to enter the parks for free, most parks more often than not become overcrowded, especially at weekends. Therefore, the beauty and peace of the parks are ruined. What's worse, now that all kinds of people are entitled to go into the parks for free, we cannot rule out the possibility of destruction, which many parks actually have already complained about.

In my opinion, citizens should not be charged to enter the parks, because as taxpayers, we deserve the right to visit parks for free. However, while we are enjoying our rights, we should also fulfill our obligations,（此处缺少逗号）such as taking good care of the parks, and maintaining the normal function of the fitness equipment.

Sample

We are well aware that current policy in China that allows free public access to most parks. This nationwide implementation of free admission aims to provide equal opportunities for individuals, regardless of their economic status, to appreciate the natural beauty and utilize the facilities within these parks.

Besides the benefits and convenience, it has also given rise to certain problems. Since people are allowed to enter the parks for free, most parks more often than not become overcrowded, especially at weekends. Therefore, the beauty and peace of the parks are ruined. What's worse, now with people from all walks of life granted free entry, the potential of destruction cannot be disregarded, which many parks actually have already complained about.

In my opinion, citizens should not be charged to enter the parks, because as tax-payers, we deserve the right to visit parks for free. However, while we are exercising our rights, we should also fulfill our obligations, such as taking good care of the parks, and maintaining the normal function of the fitness equipment.

范例3

An Australian friend has applied for a job at the company you work for. He has just written to say that he has been invited for an interview at the company next month and ask you for some advice.

Write him a letter of advice.

Write about:

• tips on how to make a good impression at the interview

• examples of questions you think he might be asked at the interview

• some background information about the people who may interview him

and any other points which you think are important.

Write at least 180 words.

Revision scheme

Dear Jack,

I am very delighted to hear that you have applied in for（此处介词使用错误）our company, and as a friend, I would also like to provide you with some reference suggestions for the interview next month to improve your success rate.

If you want to make a good impression on the interviewer, you should first dress neatly. This will make you look more like a skilled professional. Second, be polite. Because no matter what kind of people they are（此处加入 they are 因句子缺少成分）, they like to be treated with courtesy. Of course, you should also have a clear career plan, which will generally give the interviewer the impression that you are organized. Also, it is better to have some understanding of the corporate culture. This will show the company that you are sincere and that you want to work here.

The interviewer may ask you the following questions: what you think of our company, why you want to work for us, and whether you have worked in similar fields if you have any relevant work experiences（是否有相关工作经历的表达）. As long as you answer them properly, getting the job is just a piece of cake.

Your interviewer is a competent and middle-aged professional woman who likes to ask questions that are straight to the point straight-to-the-point questions（此处直接表达更简洁，不需要使用定语从句）, but if it's you, I believe you should just answer truthfully according to your own circumstances.

Good luck with your interview. I am looking forward to meeting you in the company.

Yours faithfully,
Wilson

Sample

Dear Jack,

I am very delighted to hear that you have applied for a position at our company, and as a friend, I would also like to provide you with some reference suggestions for the interview next month to improve your success rate.

If you want to make a good impression on the interviewer, it is essential to dress in a neat and professional manner. This will convey a sense of competence and expertise. Second, showing politeness towards the interviewer is crucial, as it demonstrates your respect and consideration for others. Of course, you should also have a clear career plan, which will generally give the interviewer the impression that you are organized. Moreover, it is advisable to familiarize yourself with the corporate culture, as this will showcase your interest and desire to work within the organization.

The interviewer may ask you the following questions: what you think of our company, why you want to work for us, and if you have any relevant work experiences. As long as you answer properly, getting the job is just a piece of cake.

Your interviewer is a competent and middle-aged professional woman who likes to ask straight-to-the-point questions. However, I believe that if you answer truthfully in accordance with your own circumstances, you will get a good point.

I wish you the best luck with your interview and I eagerly anticipate to meet you at our company.

Yours faithfully,
Wilson

范例4

You are a student and there is a discussion in your class on the areas which have benefited from the internet.

Write an essay for your tutor.

Write about:

· which area has benefited more from the internet

· what the importance of Internet technology is

· why you made this choice

and any other points which you think are important.

Write at least 180 words.

Revision scheme

I am writing this essay to state my opinion on which areas can benefit from Internet technology and its importance. In my opinion, the main areas benefiting from the development of the internet are education and media.

First, education has benefited most from the internet. Education is the foundation of people's livelihood and the impacts of the internet on education are most obvious. With the development of the（此处加入the，名词前的冠词不能省略）economy and affected by the epidemic, many traditional education institutions ~~begin~~ have begun （现在完成时表示过去的动作对现在的影响）to transform to online education. Through Internet technology, users' needs can be deeply mined and personalized recommendations can be realized. People can use fragmented time to learn, making online education cut a blind spot of traditional education.

Secondly, the media ~~is also greatly benefited~~ also benefits greatly（此处使用主动语态来表达更符合句意）from the internet. Traditional media is one-way information output from top to bottom, and most users passively receive information; while new media is interactive and real-time, two-way and multi-channel content dissemination, with personalized and user-friendly characteristics, which is conducive to attracting a large number of loyal and（此处加入and使表达更连贯）high-quality users.

There are much more areas in which the internet has had an impact, and I'll leave them there for lack of space. I would appreciate it very much if you would take time out of your busy schedule to ~~reply~~ respond（reply和respond均有回答的意思，但reply较为正式，respond 更合适）.

Sample

I am writing this essay to state my opinion on which areas can benefit from Internet technology and its importance. In my opinion, the main areas benefiting from the development of the internet are education and media.

First, education has benefited most from the internet. Education is the foundation of people's livelihood and the impacts of the internet on education are most obvious. With the development of the economy and the influence of the pandemic, numerous traditional education institutions have shifted towards online education. Through Internet technology, users' needs can be deeply mined and personalized recommendations can be realized. It allows individuals to engage in learning during fragmented time periods, and effectively addressing the limitations of traditional education.

Secondly, the media also benefits greatly from the internet. Traditional media primarily serves as a one-way information channel from top to bottom, leaving users in a passive role as mere recipients; while new media is interactive and real-time, two-way and multi-channel content dissemination, with personalized and user-friendly characteristics, which is conducive to attracting a great number of loyal and high-quality users.

There are much more areas in which the internet has had an impact. Unfortunately, due to space constraints, I am unable to write further details. I would appreciate it very much if you would take time out of your busy schedule to respond.

Day 6 提分篇——小短文和评论讲解

写作考试的第二部分要求考生写一篇不少于180个单词的小短文、评论、信件、意见、邮件或者帖子。与第一部分电子邮件写作的要求不同，第二部分在字数上要求得更多，需要写至少180个单词。此外，小短文、评论、信件、意见、邮件或者帖子在格式和内容上与电子邮件的要求也不相同，考生需要格外注意。本节将重点讲解小短文和评论的常用表达及例题。

一、小短文

（一）常用表达

在小短文类体裁的写作中，掌握各种意图的常用表达对考生的写作有很大的帮助，下面将对各种常用表达进行举例说明。

➡ 提出观点

1. As far as...is concerned 就……而言

2. I think that... 我认为……

3. Contrary to the popular thought，I prefer... 与普遍的想法相反，我更喜欢……

4. It goes without saying that... 不言而喻……

5. People hold different attitudes towards this issue. 人们对这一问题持有不同的态度。

6. People/Those in favour of the opinion that... 赞成……观点的人……

7. Some people...while others... 一些人……而另外一些人……

8. As far as I am concerned/ Personally 就我而言/就个人而言

9. It's hardly too much to say that... 毫不夸张地说……

10. What calls for special attention is that...需要特别注意的是……

11. Nothing is more important than the fact that... 没有什么比……更重要的了。

12. What's far more important is that... 更重要的是……

13. It can be said with certainty that... 可以肯定地说……

14. It is undeniable that... /There is no denying that... 不可否认……

15. As the proverb says 常言道

16. It is generally/ commonly believed/ recognized that... 人们普遍认为……

17. While it is commonly believed that，I believe... 虽然人们普遍认为……，但我认为……

18. It is a fact that... 事实是……

19. It is well-known that... 众所周知……

20. There is no doubt that... 毫无疑问……

➡ 内容衔接

1. A case in point is... 一个典型的例子是……

2. As is often the case... 通常情况下……

3. As stated in the previous paragraph... 如前段所述……

4. From another perspective... 从另一个角度……

5. But it's a pity that... 但遗憾的是……

6. But the problem is not so simple. Therefore... 然而问题并非如此简单，所以……

7. Undoubtedly, .../ There is no doubt that... 毫无疑问……

8. For all that... 尽管如此……

9. In spite of the fact that...尽管事实……

10. not(that)...but(that)... 不是因为……，而是因为……

11. In view of the present situation... 鉴于当前形势……

12. As has been mentioned above... 正如上面所提到的……

13. In this respect, we may as well(say) 从这个角度上我们可以（说）……

14. First/ Firstly/ In the first place/ To begin with 首先

15. Second/ Secondly/ In the second place 其次

16. Besides/ In addition/ Additionally/ Moreover/ Furthermore 再则

17. However, we have to look at the other side of the coin, which is...
然而，我们还得看到事物的另一方面，即……

18. Further, we hold the opinion that... 此外，我们坚持认为……

19. However, the difficulty lies in... 然而，困难在于……

20. Similarly, we should pay attention to... 同样，我们要注意……

→ 对观点进行说明

1. The following reasons can account for my inclination. 以下原因可以解释我的倾向。

2. I disbelieve, and therefore strongly resent the claim that... 我不相信，因此强烈反对这一主张，即……

3. For these reasons, I recommend that... 出于这些原因，我推荐/建议……

4. I'm not entirely convinced of... 我并不完全信服……

5. I cannot entirely agree with the idea that... 我无法完全同意这一观点……

6. As opposed to widely held belief, I believe that... 与普遍接受的看法不同，我认为……

7. From a personal perspective, I also prefer to... 从个人的角度来看，我也喜欢……

8. Personally, I am standing on the side of... 就个人而言，我站在……的那一边

9. There is another reason why I cast my preference for... 我倾向于……还有另外一个原因。

10. In my opinion, it is more advisable to do... than to do... 在我看来，做……比做……更明智。

11. I have nothing against..., but... 我并不反对……，但……

12. At an individual level, I feel that... 从个人的角度出发，我觉得……

13. I find the statement of... to be too narrow. 我觉得……的观点过于狭隘。

14. I can tell you from experience that... 凭经验，我可以告诉你……

15. To make myself as plain as I can, I should give my standards for... 为了使我的观点尽可能清晰，我应该把我的标准定为……。

16. From my point of view, it is more reasonable to support the first opinion rather than the others.在我看来，支持第一种观点比支持其他观点更合理。

17. My answer is that..., I have several reasons, and they're good ones. The first is the one that...
我的回答是……，我有几个理由，而且它们是很充分的理由。第一个是……

18. The situation is not rare. It is one of many examples I have encountered.
这种情况并不少见，它也是我遇到的许多情况之一。

19. Although doing... might seem a wild idea, I believe that... 虽然做……似乎很狂妄，但我相信……

20. But for me, I would rather think of the matter in an(optimistic)way. 至于我，

我宁愿以（乐观）的态度来看待这一问题。

21. In the nationwide discussion, many people suggest that.... But I argue that... 在全国范围内的讨论中，许多人建议……，但我却认为……

22. Finally, to speak frankly, there is also a more practical reason why I would choose to... 最后，坦白地讲，我选择……还有一个更为现实的原因。

23. Some people think that.... To be frank, I cannot agree with their opinion for the reasons below: 一些人认为……，坦白地讲，我不赞同他们的观点，理由如下：

24. There are some people who hold that.... And on the other hand, there are some other people who argue that.... Both opinions are very popular. But I cannot accept either view. 有一些人认为……，另一方面还有另外一些人认为……。上述两种观点都很受欢迎，但我两种观点都不能接受。

➡ 对观点进行总结

1. I will conclude by saying... 最后我要说……

2. It therefore can be said that... 因此可以说……

3. Therefore, we have the reason to believe that... 因此，我们有理由相信……

4. All things considered... 总而言之……

5. In this regard, it is fair to say that... 在这一点上，公平地说……

6. It may be safely said that... 可以有把握地说……

7. Therefore, in my opinion, it's more advisable... 因此，在我看来，更可取的是……

8. From what has been discussed above, we may safely draw the conclusion that... 综上所述，我们完全可以得出结论……

9. One can easily know this by... 通过……，就可以很容易明白这一点。

10. It is hence not difficult to see that... 因此，不难看出……

11. The data/ statistics/ figures lead us to the conclusion that... 通过数据我们得到的结论是……

12. It can be concluded from the discussion that... 从讨论中我们可以得出这样的结论……

13. From what has been discussed above, it can be concluded that... 综上所述，可以得出结论……

14. It is hence not surprising that... 因此，……也就不足为奇了。

15. From my point of view, it would be better if... 在我看来……也许更好

16. It is thus my belief that... when it comes to... 因此，说到……我坚信……

17. It can be concluded that... 可以得出结论……

➡ 对某事进行强调

1. Nothing is+形容词（比较级）+than(to do)sth. 没有比……更……的事了。

2. cannot emphasize the importance of... too much.（再怎么强调……的重要性也不为过。）

3. There is no denying that + S + V...（不可否认的是……）

4. It is universally acknowledged that + 句子（众所周知的是……）

5. There is no doubt that + 句子（毫无疑问的是……）

6. An advantage of... is that + 句子（……的优点是……）

（二）典型例题及详解

You have seen this advertisement in an online magazine.

Sport and Fitness Magazine

We would like to hear from readers who have a favourite sportsperson or sports team.
Write an article for us and we'll put the best one on our website.
Send your article to readerarticles@SFMag.com

Write an article for Sport and Fitness magazine.

Write about:

• what you know about your favourite sportsperson or team

• why you like this person or team

• what you would ask this person or team if you could meet them

and any other points you think are important.

Write at least 180 words.

观察上面的内容可以发现，题目中首先给出的是一则在线杂志广告。广告的目的是想收到人们写的关于最喜欢的运动员或运动队的文章。同时提到最好的文章将发布在杂志的官网上，还提供了接收文章的邮箱地址。

写作要求部分，首先规定了写作体裁，即 an article for Sport and Fitness magazine，考生需要为《体育与健身》杂志写一篇小短文；下面的三处二级标题是三点任务要求，考生在写作的过程中可以根据任务要求来组织文章内容，同时需要注意，在写作的过程中需要对三点任务要求分别进行说明和陈述。

下面是一篇参考范文，范文一共包括四个段落。第一段是对写作目的的概括说明，之后的三个段落是对三个要点的陈述，下面将进行详细说明。

An Essay on My Favourite Sports Teams.

This essay is about my favourite sports team—the Chinese women's national volley-ball team. In this essay I will explain how I got to know them and why I love this sports team.

通过小短文的题目读者可以对文章体裁和写作主要内容进行总体的了解；开头第一段中，作者对写作目的进行了总的说明："In this essay I will explain how I got to know them and why I love this sports team"，同时这两方面内容也是对写作任务要求的回应。

I first heard the name of the Chinese women's national volleyball team from a TV replay of the World Olympic Games. I was impressed by their constant struggle. Asians were notoriously bad at physical activities. However, with huge competition from European countries, the Chinese girls did their best to earn every point, even if in some games they finished behind some teams from European countries. Yet they never became despondent, but became more earnest in their study of the methods by which they were to compete with other teams. In the end, with a never-give-up fighting spirit, they won the competition to achieve the gold medal for China. I cried the moment they stood on the medal stand and knew that this achievement had been really hard for them, because it had been achieved through days and nights of hard practice. They are the pride of China.

正文第二段是对第一个要点的回复。在这一段中，作者详细说明了自己是如何知道中国国家女子排球队的，同时还描述了中国女排在比赛中不屈不挠并最终为中国赢得金牌的事情。在这一段的描述中，作者使用了较多的连接词，使表述更加自然流畅，如However，Yet，In the end等。考生在练习的过程中可多积累一些连接词，从而可以在考试的过程中灵活运用。

I have a feeling of reverence and awe for this striving and indomitable team. And the Chinese women's national volleyball team has achieved a lot of thanks to the great leadership of their coach Lang Ping, who is also an idol in my heart. Her spirit of hard work and tenacious perseverance has always inspired me, both in my life and studies.

正文第三段是对第二个要点的回复。在这里作者表达了对中国女排的崇敬和喜爱之情，同时还提到这支队伍所取得的成就与教练的指导有很大关系，也表达了对教练的崇敬之情，另外还提到了具体受影响的方面 "Her spirit of hard work and tenacious perseverance has always inspired me, both in my life and studies."

If I have the opportunity to meet them, I would ask them "When facing difficulties and stress from the outside, how can you deal with them?" "What do you want to say to those who are in trouble?" And I believe that their experiences can have a good influence on people who are going through a hard time.

短文最后一段是对第三个要点的回复。这个要点的内容较具体，问的是如果能见到这个团队，你会问他们什么，考生在遇到类似问题的时候，需要将思路向团队的特点方面扩展，问的问题应该能体现出团队的特征。在这篇习作中，作者问到的内容与团队的经历相关，而且他们的拼搏精神也确实对其他人有很好的影响作用，作者最后也提到，问这些问题的作用 "And I believe that their experiences can have a good influence on people who are going through a hard time."

总的来说，这篇范文是一篇很好的文章，对题目中的要点都进行了相应说明，同时对内容做到了适当的延伸，文章的整体表述也很流畅。

下面请参考完整的范文：

This essay is about my favourite sports team—the Chinese women's national volleyball team. In this essay I will explain how I got to know them and why I love this sports team.

I first heard the name of the Chinese women's national volleyball team from a TV replay of the World Olympic Games. I was impressed by their constant struggle. Asians were notoriously bad at physical activities. However, with huge competition from European countries, the Chinese girls did their best to earn every point, even if in some games they finished behind some teams from European countries. Yet they never became despondent, but became more earnest in their study of the methods by which they were to compete with other teams. In the end, with a never-give-up fighting spirit, they won the competition to achieve the gold medal for China. I cried the moment they stood on the medal stand and knew that this achievement had been really hard for them, because it had been achieved through days and nights of hard practice. They are the pride of China.

I have a feeling of reverence and awe for this striving and indomitable team. And the Chinese women's national volleyball team has achieved a lot of thanks to the great leadership of their coach Lang Ping, who is also an idol in my heart. Her spirit of hard work and tenacious perseverance has always inspired me, both in my life and studies.

If I have the opportunity to meet them, I would ask them "When facing difficulties and stress from the outside, how can you deal with them?" "What do you want to say to those who are in trouble?" And I believe that their experiences can have a good influence on people who are going through a hard time.

范文翻译：

这篇文章是关于我最喜欢的运动队——中国国家女子排球队的。在这篇文章中，我将说明我是如何知道她们的，以及我为什么喜欢这支运动队。

我第一次听到中国女排的名字是在一次世界奥运会的电视回放中。她们不断奋斗的精神给我留下了深刻的印象。众所周知，亚洲人不擅长体育活动，然而，面对与欧洲国家队伍的激烈竞争，中国女孩们尽最大努力赢得每一分。尽管在一些比赛中，她们落后于一些欧洲国家的球队，但是，她们并未气馁，而是更加认真地研究与其他团队竞技的方法。最后，凭借永不放弃的斗志，她们赢得了比赛，为中国赢得了金牌。当她们站在领奖台上的那一刻，我哭了，我知道这一成就对她们来说真的很艰难，因为这是通过日日夜夜的刻苦训练才获得的。她们是中国的骄傲。

我对这支奋斗不息、百折不挠的队伍有一种敬畏之情。中国国家女子排球队取得了很大的成就，这要感谢她们的教练郎平的精准指导，她也是我心中的偶像。无论是在生活中还是在学习中，她的勤奋和顽强的毅力一直激励着我。

如果我有机会见到她们，我会问她们："当面对来自外界的困难和压力时，你们是如何应对的？""你们想对处于困境中的人说些什么？"我相信她们的经历会对那些正处于困难时期的人产生正面的影响。

➤重点词汇及短语

---

1. favourite [ˈfeɪvərɪt] *adj.* 最喜爱的

2. national [ˈnæʃnəl] *adj.* 国家的；民族的；全国的

3. volleyball [ˈvɒlibɔːl] *n.* 排球（运动）

4. replay [ˈriːpleɪ] *n.* 重放，重演，重播

5. constant [ˈkɒnstənt] *adj.* 连续发生的；不断的；重复的

6. struggle [ˈstrʌgl] *n.* 斗争；奋斗；努力

7. notoriously [nəʊˈtɔːrɪəslɪ] *adv.* 众所周知地

8. competition [ˌkɒmpəˈtɪʃn] *n.* 竞争；比赛

9. despondent [dɪˈspɒndənt] *adj.* 苦恼的；沮丧的；泄气的

10. stand [stænd] *n.* （展示或推介物品的）桌，台，摊位

11. achievement [əˈtʃiːvmənt] *n.* 成就；成绩；功绩

12. coach [kəʊtʃ] *n.* 教练；辅导教师

13. idol [ˈaɪdl] *n.* 偶像

14. tenacious [təˈneɪʃəs] *adj.* 顽强的；坚忍不拔的

15. perseverance [ˌpɜːsəˈvɪərəns] *n.* 毅力；韧性；不屈不挠的精神

16. inspire [ɪnˈspaɪə (r)] *vt.* 激励；鼓舞

17. stress [stres] *n.* 精神压力；心理负担；紧张

18. never-give-up 永不放弃

19. gold medal 金牌；金质奖章

20. deal with 处理，应付

➤重点句型及例句

1. be impressed by... 被……所感动；被……给予深刻印象

　　例：On the Internet, you will be impressed by the video show of a girl's special commemoration.

　　在网上，一个女孩的特别纪念活动的视频节目会给你留下深刻印象。

2. compete with sb. 与某人竞争

　　例：We can't compete with them on price.

　　我们在价格上无法与他们竞争。

3. thanks to 由于，幸亏

　　例：Thanks to mobile libraries, these people can still borrow books.

　　得益于移动图书馆，这些人仍然可以借书。

二、评论

写作考试第二部分的体裁中，评论是经常出现的一种类型。写作的过程中，考生需要提出自己的观点，同时需要注意逻辑的合理性。本节将重点讲解评论的常用表达及例题。

(一) 常用表达

在评论类作文写作中，经常用到的表达包括对观点的陈述和对相关理由的论述、观点的总结，下面将对常用的表达进行总结说明。

→ 书评

1. from...to... 从……到……（表示涵盖的内容）

2. make a good case for... 很好地说明了……

3. be written specifically for... 为……专门而写的

4. make you laugh and warm your heart 让你开怀大笑，温暖你的心

5. ...is worth reading ……值得一读

6. The book is heavily marketed to... 这本书被大力推销给……

7. The basic premise of the book is that... 这本书的基本前提是……

8. ...is presenting this idea to... ……向……提出这个想法

9. Each chapter closes with... 每一章都以……结尾。

10. ... offers tremendous stories, and that's exactly what makes it so page-turning. ……提供了精彩的故事，这正是它如此引人入胜的原因

11. ...not only has a beautiful and vibrant cover, but an immersive storyline to match. ……不仅有一个漂亮的，充满活力的封面，还有让人身临其境的故事情节。

12. ... made this one of my favourite reads of the year. ……使这本书成为我今年最喜欢的读物之一。

13. She's a writer who can't be put in a box, and this is a book that readers will love. 她是一个不受束缚的作家，这是一本读者会喜欢的书。

14. Engrossing and heart pounding, this book had me on the edge of my seat from beginning to end. 引人入胜，惊心动魄，这本书从头到尾都让我紧张得要命。

15. This book features a main character you can't help but root for! 这本书的主角让你忍不住要为他加油！

16. Filled with shimmery and charismatic people who love deeply and dream

big, ... is an entirely magnetic read that you won't want to end. ……是一本让人欲罢不能的书，充满了闪闪发光、魅力四射、爱得深沉、梦想远大的人物。

→ 电影或电视剧评论

1. gripping and intense plotting 扣人心弦的情节

2. visually spectacular 视觉上很壮观

3. truly incredible performances 真正出色的表演

4. a definitive visual and heartfelt masterpiece 一部名副其实的视觉大片和发自肺腑的杰作

5. do a tremendous job narrating the story 把故事叙述得很出色

6. informative yet funny 内容丰富又有趣

7. Don't miss... 不要错过……

8. ... proves worth the wait. ……证明了等待是值得的。

9. I'm shocked with just how good... is. 我对……的出色感到震惊。

10. I can only say that I can't wait to see... 我只能说，我迫不及待地想看到……

11. A movie like this does not come around often, if at all. 像这样的电影不常出现。

12. It wants to entertain you, and to draw you in with exciting and exacting plotting. 它让人愉快，令人兴奋的、缜密的情节非常吸引人。

13. Stick with this absolute gem of a film. 一定要去看这部绝对精彩的电影。

14. Totally recommend watching it. 强烈推荐大家去看。

15. It's a profound look at family, morality, and the harshness of life. 它深刻地审视了家庭、道德和生活的残酷。

16. It is ending at exactly the appropriate moment, and these last episodes are the finest ode to what's been a fabulously funny and exquisitely-produced series. 它在恰当的时刻结束了，最后几集是对这部超级搞笑和制作精美的系列的最好颂歌。

17. The plotting overall is a bit shaggier. 整体的情节比较粗糙。

18. The ending is a bit inconsistent and has a rushed feel. 结局有点前后矛盾，给人一种仓促之感。

19. I was by turns irritated and bored when watching it. 看它的时候，我时而恼火，时而厌烦。

20. I was expecting so much better with this team. 我对这支制作团队的期望远不止如此。

21. It's not terrible, but that's about the only compliment I can give it. 它并不糟糕，但这是我能给它的唯一赞美。

22. Unfortunately, it's easy enough to see where the twists and turns are going to take us. 遗憾的是，我们很容易能看出剧中的变化和转折的结局。

23. I just wish it had been given more time to tell a complete story, with a perceptible middle, beginning and end.

我只是希望它能有更多的时间来讲述一个完整的故事，有一个可以理解的起因、经过与结果。

→ 饭馆或餐厅评论

1. hospitable hosts, delicious dishes, beautiful presentation, wide menu list and wonderful dessert 好客的主人，美味的菜肴，漂亮的外观，丰富的菜单和美妙的甜点

2. huge variety of dishes to choose from 种类繁多的菜肴可供选择

3. I have to say, I enjoyed every single bite of the meal in... 我不得不说，我很享受在······吃的这顿饭的每一口。

4. Definitely a go-to place for... when you are in... 当你在······的时候，一定要去······

5. Food is pretty good. 食物很不错。

6. The food is absolutely amazing. 这里的食物太棒了。

7. Everything is so tasty, you cannot restraint yourself from having all of the dishes. 每样东西都很好吃，你无法控制自己不吃所有的菜。

8. Menu is extensive and seasonal to a particularly high standard. 菜单的选择范围很广泛，食材都是高标准应季的。

9. The service we received was so amazing. 我们得到的服务太棒了。

10. They made us feel welcomed and gave us an amazing experience. 他们让我们有宾至如归的感觉，并给了我们一次难忘的体验。

11. The ambiance is very welcoming and charming. 这里的氛围非常温馨迷人。

12. The staff is really friendly. 员工都很友好。

13. The staff truly cares about your experience. 员工真正关心的是您的体验。

14. Waiters are very attentive. 服务员很细心。

15. Servers are also great and always efficient, happy and polite. 服务员也很好，总是很有效率，令人愉快又有礼貌。

16. The service is unmatched. 服务无与伦比。

17. Service was delightful and very professional. 服务很好，也很专业。

18. Can't wait to return and wouldn't hesitate to recommend to anyone looking for somewhere to eat in. 等不及要再来了，会毫不犹豫地推荐给任何想找地方吃饭的人。

19. This is my absolute favourite restaurant. 这绝对是我最喜欢的餐厅。

20. This place is great! 这个地方太棒了！

21. I would like to come back here again and again. 我想一次又一次地来这里。

22. We will definitely be back again. 我们一定会再来的。

23. The meals were served rapidly and the rates were reasonable. 饭菜上得很快，价格也很合理。

24. Do yourself a favour and visit this lovely restaurant. 对自己好点儿，去看看这家可爱的餐厅吧。

25. This spot gives extraordinary service and yummy meals. 这个地方提供非凡的服务和美味的饭菜。

26. Great place to hangout，chill or go out on a date. 是闲逛、放松或约会的好地方。

27. Definitely a lifetime customer! 我绝对是终身顾客！

➡ 旅馆或酒店评论

1. ... made our stay most memorable. ……使我们的住宿经历很难忘。

2. I recently had the pleasure of staying at..., and it was an unforgettable experience. 我最近有幸住在……，那是一次难忘的经历。

3. My stay at... was nothing short of spectacular. 我在……的住宿经历简直是棒极了。

4. With its convenient location and outstanding service，... has quickly become my go-to choice for accommodations whenever I travel to the area. 凭借其便利的地理位置和出色的服务，……已迅速成为无论何时我到该地区的首选住宿地。

5. The room was perfect. 房间很完美。

6. Everything was of top standard. 一切都是顶级标准。

7. The room was clean and bright，and the room service was always on time. 房间干净明亮，客房服务总是很准时。

8. The luxurious accommodations，coupled with exceptional service，made my stay truly memorable. 豪华的住宿，加上卓越的服务，使我的住宿经历相当难忘。

9. The hotel's prime location made exploring the city a breeze. 这家旅馆的绝佳位

153

置使游览这座城市变得轻而易举。

10. The hotel's elegant design, combined with its top-notch amenities, made for a truly relaxing and enjoyable experience. 酒店优雅的设计，结合其一流的设施，给了我一个真正的放松和愉快的体验。

➡ 商店或商场评论

1. lively and fun 充满活力又有趣

2. very knowledgeable in addressing questions 见多识广，有问必答

3. use the mobile app to pay 使用手机应用程序支付

4. ... is a great place to... ……是一个……的好去处。

5. I was especially pleased to... 我特别高兴……

6. I'll be going to... from now on. 从现在开始我会去……

7. I'll keep going to... 我会一直去……

8. Overall, my experience with... was outstanding, and I can't wait for my next purchase. 总的来说，我在……的体验非常好，我已经等不及再一次购买了。

9. I'm really pleased with... 我对……非常满意。

10. I've always been satisfied with... 我对……一直很满意。

11. This initial experience with... was utterly gratifying and I'm looking forward to the next visit. 在……的初次体验让我非常满意，我期待着下次光顾。

12. I'm thrilled with the quality and will definitely shop at... again in the future. 我对它的质量很满意，将来一定会再来……购物。

13. The quality is remarkable. 质量非常好。

14. The owner was very nice. 店主人非常好。

15. They are high-quality and worth the money. 它们质量上乘，物有所值。

16. Their support team responded promptly and professionally. 他们的支持团队迅速而专业地做出了回应。

➡ 电子产品商店评论

1. I did plenty of researches on several places before choosing... 在选择……之前，我对几个地方做了大量的研究。

2. I've bought many phones through... over the years, and have never been disappointed. 这些年来，我通过……买了很多手机，从来没有失望过。

3. It's always a smooth and easy process purchasing from here. 从这里购物总是一个顺利、简单的过程。

4. The phone was in perfect condition and came very quickly, safely packaged. 手机状况很好，到货迅速，包装完好。

5. Shipping is fast，and the phone condition is always as expected，with no surprises. 发货速度快，手机的状况总是如预期的那样，没有任何意外。

6. It's so much better than other shops at finding exactly what you need. 在找到你需要的东西方面，它比其他商店好得多。

7. Customer service responds very quickly. 客服的反应非常快。

8. Thorough information was given about the product. There were no ambiguities. （店员）提供了有关该产品的详细信息，没有任何含糊之处。

9. The payment system worked well. 支付系统运行良好。

10. I wouldn't hesitate to buy from this seller again in the future! 我以后还会毫不犹豫地从这个卖家处买东西！

11. I bought a MacBook Pro 2021 with no issues and got everything as described. 我买了一台MacBook Pro 2021，没有任何问题，一切都和描述的一样。

12. The item was exactly what I was looking for, at an excellent price. 这件东西正是我所要找的，价格公道。

13. Communication was prompt and clear，and the product looked more beautiful than expected. 沟通迅速而且清晰，产品看起来比预期的漂亮。

14. Everything was quick and responsive. 一切都很快，有求必应。

15. I can't complain at all with how fast，easy，and efficient everything was. 一切都是那么快速、简单和高效，我没有什么可挑剔的。

➡ 在线购物评论

1. stylish and comfortable 时尚又舒适

2. I would recommend... to everyone. 我会向所有人推荐……

3. I highly recommend... 我强烈推荐……

4. I recommend... to anyone looking for ... 我向寻找……的人推荐……

5. ... is perfect for... 对于……来说，……是完美的。

6. ... is always our first option and it never disappoints. ……永远是我们的第一选择，而且从来不会让人失望。

7. I recently discovered... while searching for a specific... 我最近在寻找……（商品名）时发现了……（店名）。

8. The...arrived in excellent condition，exactly as described on their website. ……

完好无损，和他们网站上描述的一模一样。

9. Highly recommend! 强烈推荐!

10. More variety would be nice. 种类再多一些就好了。

11. We were especially pleased with the prompt delivery. 我们对及时送货特别满意。

12. I was amazed at how quickly it arrived. 我惊讶于它到货如此之快。

13. Considering the quality, the price is reasonable. 考虑到质量，这个价格是合理的。

14. There was only one minor problem in the purchasing process. 在购买过程中只有一个小问题。

15. The packaging was secure, ensuring the item was undamaged. 包装完好，确保物品没有损坏。

16. Their website was user-friendly, making it easy to find the perfect item. 他们的网站对用户很友好，很容易找到合适的商品。

17. The checkout process was smooth, and I received my order promptly. 结账过程很顺利，我很快就收到了我订购的货品。

18. The website was easy to navigate, and the product descriptions were informative and accurate. 网站易于浏览，产品描述信息详细且准确。

19. I was pleasantly surprised by the fast shipping and the care they took in packaging my order. 我对快速的运输和他们对我的订单的包装感到惊喜。

（二）典型例题及详解

You have seen this advertisement in an online culture magazine.

> Have you been to a concert, show, or performance recently? Why not write in and tell us about it? The best reviews will be published online!
>
> Send your review to: reviews@discoverculture.com

Write a review for Modern Culture magazine.

Write about:

• what you saw at the concert, show, or performance

• who the other people at the concert, show, or performance were

• whether you would recommend the concert, show, or performance

and any other points you think are important.

Write at least 180 words.

观察题目可以发现，题目中给出的是一则在线广告。结合广告中的内容可以了解到，一家在线文化杂志希望收到人们对于音乐会或演出的评价，同时提供了接收评论的邮箱地址。

广告下方对写作体裁和写作要求进行了说明。"a review for Modern Culture magazine." 是对写作体裁的说明，考生需要写一篇评论。下面的三处二级标题列出了三点任务要求，分别为：你在音乐会、演出或表演中看到了什么；还有谁参加了音乐会、演出或表演；以及你是否会推荐这场音乐会、演出或表演。考生在写评论的过程中需要对这三方面的内容进行说明，同时在对第三点任务进行说明的过程中，还需要给出自己的观点。

下面是一篇参考范文，范文一共包括五个段落。第一段是对自己参加的一次音乐会进行的总结概括，之后的四个段落是对三个要点的陈述，下面将进行详细说明。

I'd like to write this review to talk about a thrilling and memorable concert I've recently been to, which I would recommend to everyone.

第一段中作者对自己的写作目的进行了说明，并对音乐会进行了描述 "a thrilling and memorable concert"，同时表达出愿意将音乐会推荐给所有人 "which I would recommend to everyone"。

The concert was a Beach House concert in a live house in Shanghai. If you're a fan of indie music or dream pop, you've probably heard of Beach House, as they're one of the most well-known dream pop bands. At the concert, I saw the vocalist Victoria Legrand and the guitarist Alex Scally. The room was dark, and the stage was bathed in multicoloured clouds of smoke rising up and obscuring their faces. Legrand had a mysterious presence, swaying along to the haunting ambient music. Her voice was so rich and hypnotic, and the sounds emanating from Scally's guitar were magnificent.

第二段是对题目要求中第一个要点的回复，在这里作者对音乐会演出的地点、演奏人员、演奏时的环境以及声音进行了描述。本段有一句对环境的描述比较生动 "The room was dark, and the stage was bathed in multicoloured clouds of smoke rising up and obscuring their faces." 使读者有身临其境的感觉。

There were many other people at the concert, including a few of my friends from our university. Most people were probably in their twenties or thirties and clearly fans of indie music. I remember some people even wore Beach House T-shirts, and a lot of the concertgoers had dyed hair, piercings, and a unique fashion style. They looked like quite an artistic and unconventional crowd of people, as were my friends. During the concert, my friends and I were near the front of the stage, so it was an incredible, up-close-and-personal experience.

第三段是对题目要求中第二个要点的回复，对参加音乐会的其他人员进行了描述说明。这段中对人们的描述包括年龄描述 "Most people were probably in their twenties or thirties and clearly fans of indie music." 同时还描述了他们的衣着和打扮 "some people even wore Beach House T-shirts, and a lot of the concertgoers had dyed hair, piercings, and a unique fashion style" 这些描述可以体现音乐会观众的特征。

To wrap things up, I'd certainly recommend a Beach House concert to anyone, since they are one-of-a-kind. Not only were the vocals and performance spectacular, but also the stage design and the overall atmosphere. It's like you were fully immersed in an otherworldly experience, and Legrand's voice really leaves you breathless.

Thus, if you ever have the opportunity, I highly recommend you attend a Beach House concert.

最后两段是对题目要求中第三个要点的回复，其实在文章的第一段作者已经表明了自己的观点，会向所有人推荐这场音乐会，在最后两段中，作者详细说明了自己推荐的原因。作者在第四段开头进行了概括性说明 "I'd certainly recommend a Beach House concert to anyone, since they are one-of-a-kind." 接下来详细说明了为什么是独一无二的，分别提到了人声、表演、舞台设计和整体氛围。

最后一段中作者再次强调了自己的观点 "I highly recommend you attend a Beach House concert." 进行了很好的收尾。

整篇文章结构紧凑，对要点进行了详细的说明，对场景的描述也非常生动形象，是一篇非常好的评论。

下面请参考完整的范文：

I'd like to write this review to talk about a thrilling and memorable concert I've recently been to, which I would recommend to everyone.

The concert was a Beach House concert in a live house in Shanghai. If you're a fan of indie music or dream pop, you've probably heard of Beach House, as they're one of the most well-known dream pop bands. At the concert, I saw the vocalist Victoria Legrand and the guitarist Alex Scally. The room was dark, and the stage was bathed in multicoloured clouds of smoke rising up and obscuring their faces. Legrand had a mysterious presence, swaying along to the haunting ambient music. Her voice was so rich and hypnotic, and the sounds emanating from Scally's guitar were magnificent.

There were many other people at the concert, including a few of my friends from our university. Most people were probably in their twenties or thirties and clearly fans of indie music. I remember some people even wore Beach House T-shirts, and a lot of the concertgoers had dyed hair, piercings, and a unique fashion style. They seemed like quite an artistic and unconventional crowd of people, as were my friends. During the concert, my friends and I were near the front of the stage, so it was an incredible, up-close-and-personal experience.

To wrap things up, I'd certainly recommend a Beach House concert to anyone, since they are one-of-a-kind. Not only were the vocals and performance spectacular, but also the stage design and the overall atmosphere. It was like you were fully immersed in an otherworldly experience, and Legrand's voice really leaves you breathless.

Thus, if you ever have the opportunity, I highly recommend you attend a Beach House concert.

范文翻译：

我想写这篇评论来谈谈我最近听过的一场激动人心、令人难忘的音乐会，我会向所有人推荐这场音乐会。

这场音乐会是Beach House在上海的一个现场演唱会。如果你是独立音乐或梦幻流行音乐的粉丝，你可能听说过Beach House，因为他们是最著名的梦幻流行乐队之一。在音乐会上，我看到了主唱维多利亚·勒格兰和吉他手亚历克斯·斯卡利。房间里很暗，舞台搭建于绚彩的烟雾之中，上升的烟雾遮住了他们的脸庞。勒格兰神秘登场，随着令人难忘的背景音乐摇摆。她的声音是如此富有层次且令人陶醉，从斯卡利的吉他中发出的声音也使人大为惊叹。

音乐会上还有很多人，包括我大学时的几个朋友。大多数人可能都是二三十岁的年轻人，显然是独立音乐的粉丝。我记得有些人甚至穿着Beach House的T恤，很多参加音乐会的人染了头发，打了耳洞，穿着风格前卫时尚。他们似乎是一群很有艺术天分、不走寻常路的人，我的朋友们也是如此。在音乐会期间，我和我的朋友们都靠近舞台前面，所以这是一次不可思议的近距离体验。

总结一下，我当然会向所有人推荐一场Beach House音乐会，因为他们是独一无二的。不仅是主唱和表演令人惊叹，舞台设计和整体氛围也非常盛大。就像你完全沉浸在另一个世界中，勒格兰的声音真的让你屏气凝神。

因此，如果你有机会，我强烈推荐你去参加Beach House的音乐会。

➢ 重点词汇及短语

---

1. thrilling ['θrɪlɪŋ] *adj.* 令人兴奋的；毛骨悚然的

2. memorable ['memərəbl] *adj.* 值得纪念的；显著的，难忘的；重大的

3. live [laɪv] *adj.* 活的；现场直播的

4. fan [fæn] *n.* 迷；狂热爱好者；狂热仰慕者

5. indie ['ɪndi] *adj.* 独立的

6. probably ['prɒbəbli] *adv.* 几乎肯定；很可能；大概

7. vocalist ['vəukəlɪst] *n.* 声乐家；歌手

8. guitarist [gɪ'tɑːrɪst] *n.* 吉他弹奏者

9. multicoloured [ˈmʌltɪˌkʌləd] *adj.* 多彩的，彩色的

10. mysterious [mɪ'stɪəriəs] *adj.* 神秘的，诡秘的

11. ambient ['æmbiənt] *adj.* 周围的，环境的

12. hypnotic [hɪp'nɒtɪk] *adj.* 有催眠作用的；使人昏昏欲睡的

13. dye [daɪ] *vt.* 给……染色；染

14. unconventional [ˌʌnkən'venʃənl] *adj.* 不因循守旧的；不因袭的；新奇的

15. crowd [kraʊd] *n.* 人群；观众

16. incredible [ɪn'kredəbl] *adj.* 不可思议的；惊人的；难以置信的

17. spectacular [spek'tækjələ (r)] *adj.* 壮观的；壮丽的；令人惊叹的

18. otherworldly [ˌʌðə'wɜːldli] *adj.* 非现实世界的，超世俗的，超自然的

➢ 重点句型及例句

1. recommend sth. to sb. 向某人推荐某物

例：I recommend the book to all my students.

我向我所有的学生都推荐这本书。

2. was bathed in... 沐浴于……；被……笼罩

例：The castle was bathed in moonlight.

城堡沐浴在月光里。

三、常见话题

领思通用考试的写作题目大多来自日常生活，考生在平时的学习中需要掌握相关问题的回答思路及方向，从而可以在有限的考试时间内快速对题目做出全面的回答，并获得高分。下面将针对第二部分写作中可能出现的话题进行列举，并对常见的回答方向和

常用表达进行简要说明。

第二部分的题目形式有很多种，其中常见的一种形式是要求考生根据网站上发布的公告或广告写出自己的评论或文章：

对网站内容进行评论 ｛ 对官方网站上的内容进行评论
　　　　　　　　　　　 对商业网站上的内容进行评论

官方网站上经常涉及的内容 ｛ 城镇汽车和卡车流量增加
　　　　　　　　　　　　　　城镇街道上的垃圾增多
　　　　　　　　　　　　　　建主题公园

➡ 汽车和卡车流量增加的原因

✦ A 40-block building is being constructed in our neighborhood.

✦ More and more families own their cars.

✦ The main road that leads to the center of the city is banned for decoration of the coming festival, so people whose workplaces are located in the center have no choice but to drive through our town to their work everyday.

➡ 汽车和卡车流量增加带来的影响

✦ Citizens may not only endure the noise that is made by the vehicles, but also suffer from illnesses caused by air pollution.

✦ People cannot sleep well at night.

✦ Things in the outside are dusty because of carelessly covered containers of the lorries.

✦ be late for work and school because of traffic jams

城镇街道上的垃圾增多 ｛ 垃圾增多的原因
　　　　　　　　　　　　带来的问题
　　　　　　　　　　　　减少垃圾的方法

➡ 垃圾增多的原因

✦ lack of public attention

✦ People become too lazy and careless to pick up their own trash.

✦ When students are in their summer holidays, they like to relax by hosting parties; a lot of the cigarettes, soda cans, beer bottles and plastic cups they use are ending up on the streets.

✦ without strict law enforcement against littering

➡ 带来的问题

✦ The piles of trash on the streets are dirty and unsightly; the entire town becomes a less pleasant environment to live in.

✦ Excessive amounts of littering can be extremely detrimental to the environment.

✦ Trash releases harmful greenhouse gases that endanger the air and atmosphere.

✦ Negative impacts on ecosystems and wildlife; animals might ingest the inedible materials.

➡ 减少垃圾的方法

✦ public attention; campaigns to address the hazards of littering

✦ strict law enforcement; penalties should be implemented

建主题公园 ⎨ 在当地建主题公园是否适合
公园的建成对当地的影响
其他替代方案

➡ 在当地建主题公园是否适合

✦ the combination of architectural styles

✦ the financial impact of the construction costs

➡ 公园的建成对当地的影响

✦ increase in tourism to the town

✦ traffic congestion to local residents

✦ The increase in tourism will also have a negative effect on the environment.

➡ 其他替代方案

✦ replace the theme park with a normal park

✦ provide more body building apparatus in public places

商业网站上经常涉及的内容 ⎨ 评论去过的体育中心/休闲中心
评论看过的电影
评论学校是否应该停止供应午餐

评论去过的体育/休闲中心 ⎨ 体育/休闲中心的位置/交通情况
提供的设施/能进行的活动
开放时间
客户群/人流量

➡ 体育/休闲中心的位置/交通情况

✦ located beside the river/ in the center of the CBD

- ✦ located less than a mile from the town center

- ✦ easy to access

- ✦ a bus stop right at the entrance

- ✦ There is a large car park.

- ✦ You can go on foot or even drive or take the bus if you prefer.

➡ 提供的设施/能进行的活动

- ✦ four large indoor basketball courts

- ✦ The facilities are very modern.

- ✦ The gym has the most up-to-date equipment for a really good workout.

- ✦ full gym facilities

- ✦ three fitness studios

- ✦ a heated indoor swimming pool/ a sauna and showers

- ✦ There are two tournaments twice every year.

➡ 开放时间

- ✦ It is open seven days a week, from 6:00 a.m. to 9:00 p.m..

- ✦ open five days a week from Monday to Friday

- ✦ 24-hour opening on Fridays and Saturdays

➡ 客户群/人流量

- ✦ The main group is the young people.

- ✦ There are some facilities suitable for the teenagers.

- ✦ All the trainers are really professional.

评论看过的电影 { 说明喜欢的影片类型
说明喜欢在家看电影还是在影院
说明喜欢自己看电影还是跟朋友一起
对看过的电影进行描述

➡ 说明喜欢的影片类型

- ✦ comedy/ adventure/ fantasy/ mystery/ thriller/ war/ romance/ horror/ action/ crime

➡ 说明喜欢在家看电影还是在影院

- ✦ The viewing facilities in the cinema are very professional and the sound effect is better.

- ✦ Going to the cinema to see a movie can experience more directly the reality and existence of the movie, and can be more integrated into the play.

✦ It's cheaper to watch movies at home.

✦ You can feel more comfortable to watch movies at home without the disturb of others.

➡ 说明喜欢自己看电影还是跟朋友一起

✦ share the happiness from the movies with your friends

✦ exchange views about the film

✦ Watching a movie on your own is better for thinking.

➡ 对看过的电影进行描述

✦ It's a psychological drama and it's set in a New York music academy.

✦ The film tells a moving story of...

✦ For me, the best aspect of the film was the...

学校是否应该停止供应午餐 ⎰ 说明学校为学生提供午餐能带来的好处
                          说明不提供午餐带来的影响
                          在食品的选择上提供建议

➡ 说明学校为学生提供午餐带来的好处

✦ Lunch is the main meal of the day and students can rely on it to absorb the nutrition they need.

✦ We all know how hungry children get so it's important they are offered a meal in the middle of the day.

✦ It is very convenient for students to have lunch at school.

✦ Parents don't have to worry about their children while they are having lunch at school.

➡ 说明不提供午餐带来的影响

✦ Students would find it hard to concentrate in the afternoon.

✦ Students have to have the meal outside school; not safe nor healthy.

✦ a waste of the rest time

✦ Parents have to prepare food for their children.

➡ 在食品的选择上提供建议

✦ healthy food cooked by professional chefs

✦ no fried food or fast food

✦ vegetables and fish

✦ a good combination of fruit and vegetables

除了上面列出的对网站上发布的公告或广告内容进行评论的题目形式外，有些题目会直接要求对某些观点进行描述或评论，下面的题目要求对未来的某些方面进行说明。

对未来的描述 { 未来的教育
未来的旅行方式
未来的学校

对未来的教育的描述 { 教育方式
教学内容
与现在的教育相比的优缺点

➜ 教育方式

✦ Online teaching is more common.

✦ more convenient in terins of terms planning

✦ with the application of more advanced equipment

➜ 教学内容

✦ closer to real life

✦ pay more attention to practice

✦ pay more attention to interest cultivation

➜ 与现在的教育相比的优缺点

✦ more convenient for learning

✦ It is convenient to teach students according to their aptitude.

✦ It is inconvenient for students to improve their feelings.

对未来的旅行方式的描述 { 与当今的旅游相比，不会变的方面有哪些
与当今的旅游业相比，不同点是什么

➜ 不会变的方面有哪些

✦ People's desire and demand for tourism remain unchanged.

✦ When people have a long holiday, going out to travel is still the first choice for entertainment and leisure.

➜ 不同点是什么

✦ Current travel mode is based on tour groups; in the future, people will choose to drive more.

✦ pay more attention to immersive experience

✦ People will be immersed in an elaborately created atmosphere to form a new scene experience.

✦ Future tourism will pay more attention to meet the needs of different tourists through humanistic services.

未来的学校 $\left\{\begin{array}{l}\text{未来的学校与现在的学校的区别}\\\text{学生能体验到的内容}\\\text{说明优缺点}\end{array}\right.$

➡ 未来的学校与现在的学校的区别

✦ The teaching facilities are more advanced.

✦ pay attention to the cultivation of students' personality

✦ The teaching methods focus more on individual acceptance.

➡ 学生能体验到的内容

✦ Interest can be developed better.

✦ be exposed to more high-tech experiences

➡ 说明优缺点

✦ have the opportunity to access to high technology

✦ more opportunities to express one's interest and develop it into a career

四、常用功能表达句

在对各类话题进行表述的过程中，考生可以使用一些常用的功能表达语句，从而增强语言表达能力和文章整体的流畅性，下面将列举出一些常用的功能表达句供考生参考和记忆。

(一) 表达想要做某事的意愿

- I am really looking forward to discussing... with you. 我很期待和您探讨……
- We expect... this year. 我们期待今年……
- I expect to earn at least... a year. 我希望一年最少能挣……
- I would rather... than... 我宁可……，也不会……
- I'd like to express my appreciation for... 我想要对……表示感谢。
- I'd like to take this idea a step further. 我进一步深化这一思想。
- We hope you can see our point of view. 我们希望您能理解我们的想法。
- We want to take more of the.... 我们想占有更多的……
- I was hoping for a lower price. 我希望价格再低点。

（二）说明计划和决定

- We are also planning to negotiate with local authorities on... problem. 我们也计划与当地政府商讨……问题。

- I intend to apply for the post of... 我打算申请……一职。

- The supermarket will be closed for the month of... 超市将在……月关闭。

- I plan to send a mass e-mail to... 我准备给……群发电子邮件。

- I decide to start my own business. 我决定自己开公司了。

（三）对观点进行表达

询问观点

- What do you think? 您怎么看？

- What's your opinion on this? 您对此有何意见？

- What's your view on this? 您对此有何看法？

- Do you agree with me? 您同意我的看法吗？

- What do you think of the new...? 您认为新……怎么样？

- What do you suggest we do about this? 您对我们应该怎么做有什么建议吗？

相当肯定地表达观点

- I definitely think that... is usually the winner. 我一直认为……说了算。

- I'm absolutely sure that... 我敢肯定……

- I'm certain that you'd be... 我认为您会是……

- I firmly believe that there's a fairly easy way to improve the process. 我坚信有比较简单的改进流程的方法。

- I really feel this new product will be really popular. 我确信这个新产品将会非常畅销。

语气一般地表达观点

- I don't think it would be sensible for us to... 我认为我们……不明智。

- I think we should postpone... 我想我们应该推迟……

- I'm sure it will be... 这一定……

- In my opinion, it might be better if... 依我看，……会更好些。

- I believe you'd be the... 我觉得您会是……

- I think your figure should stay the same. 我认为你们的数字应该维持不变。

- In my view, 6% is a little high. 要我说，6%有点高了。

（四）做出保证

- I can reassure you that... 我能向您保证，……

- The government has promised... 政府已承诺……

- We are committed to..., no matter what it takes. 我们保证……，不管代价是什么。

- I can assure you, service on items we sell won't be a problem. 我敢向您保证，我们的售后服务绝对没问题。

（五）建议和劝告

征求意见和建议

- Can I ask your advice about...? 您能帮我出出关于……的主意吗？

- Do you want to go to... and... if time permits? 如果时间允许，你想去……和……吗？

- Have you thought of doing...? 您考虑过……吗？

- Shall I organize a/ an...on Saturday? 我周六组织一个……怎样？

- We could consider doing... 我们可以考虑……

- You could ask...if he wants to come. 您可以问……是否愿意来。

- Shall we start right into our meeting? 现在我们的会议可以开始吗？

- What do you think I should do? 您认为我该怎么做？

- How about...? ……如何？

提供意见或建议

- I suggest you... 我建议您……

- I think you should... 我想您应该……

- I'd recommend you to... 我建议您……

- If I were you, I would... 如果我是您，我会……

- Try to be more prepared next time. 下回准备更充分些。

- What if I talked to...? 我和……谈谈怎样？

- Why don't we do a...? 我们何不做一个……？

- Why not give him a call? 为什么不给他打个电话？

- You had better use a/ an... 您最好用一个……

- You need to start with the... 您需要从……入手。
- You ought to get the... serviced. 您该把……拿去修了。
- You should have a word with... 您应该和……好好谈谈。

(六) 征求许可

- Can I change it to an earlier flight? 我可不可以改订早一点的航班？
- Can I use this card to get some cash in advance? 我可以用这张卡来预支现金吗？
- Could I possibly borrow your...? 我能借用您的……吗？
- Do you mind if I...? 我……可以吗？
- Would you mind if I were（虚拟语气）with you to the...? 我跟您一起去……可以吗？

(七) 提出请求

- Please return the... to us. 请将……退给我们。
- Can you deliver them...? 你们可以把它们送到……吗？
- Can you give me a hand with...? 您能帮助我做……吗？
- Will you offer any more of a discount? 您能再给一些折扣吗？
- Will you send me... by e-mail? 您能把……用电子邮件发给我吗？
- Would you mind scanning in... for me? 您是否介意将……扫描给我？
- I wonder if you would forward this letter to...? 能把这封信转给……吗？
- I was wondering if you could...? 我想知道您能否……？
- Please make... by July 5. 请在7月5日前……

(八) 表达喜欢和兴趣

- I fancy a job in.... 我喜欢……方面的工作。
- I like the fact that.... 我喜欢……
- I prefer... to.... 相较于……，我更喜欢……
- I'm extremely interested in.... 我对……尤其感兴趣。
- I'm not very fond of... 我并不喜欢……
- I'm not very keen on... films. 我并不喜欢……的影片。
- I dislike... and plan to... as soon as possible. 我不喜欢……，打算尽快……
- I'm comfortable working under deadlines. 我可以在截止日期前轻松完成工作。

（九）表示惊讶

• I was astonished that he... 他竟然……，这让我大为惊讶。

• I was surprised to hear that.... 听说……我很惊讶。

• I'd be surprised to see... 如果看到……，我会感到奇怪。

• His sudden resignation came as a complete shock to me. 他突然辞职对我来说如同晴天霹雳。

（十）表达可能性

• He can be wrong to say so. 他这么说可能错了。

• It could be... before we get a reply. 我们可能要……后得到答复。

• Our biggest rival might be... 我们最大的竞争对手恐怕要算……了。

• There may not be enough money to pay for the... ……费可能不够。

• We must become more competitive if we can hold on to our strategy of... 如果我们保持……策略就一定要具有更强的竞争力。

• You must be from the...? 您一定是从……来的吧?

（十一）说明时间、频率、速度

时间

• I heard your flight was delayed by over... hours. 我听说您的飞机晚点了……个多小时。

• If we leave at 9:30, we should be able to get there by 12:40. 如果我们9:30出发，我们应该能在12:40之前到那儿。

• My job interview is at 2:30 p.m. this Monday. 我的工作面试时间是这周一下午2:30。

频率

• He frequently goes to... on business trips. 他经常去……出差。

• I usually check my e-mail about... times a day. 我通常一天要查看……次电子邮件。

• The doctor said I should take the medicine... a day. 医生说这种药我应该一天吃……次。

时间段

• I've been working as a... for... years. 我已做了……年的……

• Over the past year we have sold... mobile phones. 过去一年我们共售出……部手机。

• The flights are a bit pricey at this time of the year. 每年的这个时候机票都会比较贵。

速度

• ... managed to finish it in only... ……只用了……就完成了。

• I was driving at... km/h when... ……的时候，我开车的时速达到了……公里。

• One of my friends can read over... words a minute. 我有个朋友一分钟能看……多个字。

• The new high-speed train has a maximum speed of... km/h. 这种新型高速列车的最高时速可以达到每小时……公里。

（十二）说明距离

• I live roughly... kilometers from the CBD. 我住的地方距中央商务区大约有……公里。

• It'll take us just over... hours to get there by train. 我们坐火车到那里需要……个多小时。

• The museum is about... kilometers away from the subway station. 那家博物馆距地铁站大约……公里。

• We live about a...-minute drive from each other. 我们两个住的地方相距大约……分钟的车程。

（十三）说明金钱

• After switching jobs, his monthly salary jumped from... to... 换工作后，他的月收入从……涨到……

• Her company suffered a net loss of... last year. 她的公司去年净亏损……

• His income last year totalled approximately... 他去年的总收入接近……

• I bought a new bicycle in China for... 我在中国花……买了一辆新的自行车。

• In some countries, sales tax is included in marked prices. 在一些国家，商品的标价包含销售税。

（十四）说明质地

• I bought all the ingredients needed to make a cherry pie. 我买了制作樱桃派需要的所有原料。

• I prefer matte finish photographs to glossy ones. 比起光面照片我更喜欢亚光的。

• I want to buy some mahogany furniture. 我想买一些红木家具。

• I'm attaching a high-resolution image of our revised corporate brochure. 通过附件发给您一份我公司新的宣传册的图片，该图片是高分辨率的。

• Please make sure to print the letters on... cotton paper. 请用含棉……的纸打印这封信。

• The greeting cards I bought are made from 80% recycled paper. 我买的贺卡80%是用再生纸做的。

• Their new house was constructed primarily of glass and steel. 他们的新房子主要是用玻璃和钢材建造的。

Day 7　提分篇——其他

除了上个章节中讲到的小短文和评论两种体裁外，领思通用考试第二部分的写作题目还会出现信件、意见、邮件或者帖子等体裁的写作。邮件的写作方法在第一部分中已经进行了详细的说明，考生可以参考第一部分的内容对邮件的写作格式和常用表达进行了解，这部分不再做详细说明。本节将重点讲解剩下三种体裁的写作方法。

一、意见

（一）常用表达

在表述意见的过程中，常常涉及对观点的陈述，除了下面列出的意见的常用表达外，考生在写作的过程中，还可以参考小短文和评论章节中列出的常用表达，并进行灵活运用。

1. In my opinion... 我的意见是……

2. I think/ believe that... 我觉得/相信……

3. If you ask me..., I would say... 如果你问我……，我会说……

4. The point is that... 重点是……

5. As far as I'm concerned... 就我而言……

6. I'd like to say this... 我要说的是……

7. What I mean to say was... 我的意思是说……

8. I reckon it will be... 我估计会是……

9. It seems to me... 在我看来……

10. All things considered, I think... 综合考虑，我认为……

11. To be honest/ To tell you the truth/ To be frank, ... 说实话/说老实话/坦白地说……

12. Frankly speaking, I don't... 坦率地说，我不……

13. Personally, I think... 我个人认为……

14. To my mind... 在我看来……

（二）典型例题及详解

Your local school is thinking about discontinuing school lunches. You are concerned that this will impact students' health and decide to leave a comment on the school website.

Write your comments on the school website.

Write about:

- why lunch is so important for students
- the benefits of having lunch at school
- how school meals could be cheaper and healthier

and any other points you think are important.

Write at least 180 words.

观察上面的内容可以了解到，当地学校正在考虑停止提供午餐。你担心这会影响学生的健康，决定在学校网站上留言。

写作要求部分对体裁和内容要求进行了说明：考生需要写一篇意见；文章内容要体现三个方面，分别为：午餐重要的原因、学校提供午餐的好处、使学校膳食更便宜、更健康的方法，考生可以根据这三方面来组织文章内容。

下面是一篇参考范文，一共包含四个段落。分别从题目要求中的三个方面对观点进行了说明。范文的详细说明如下。

I am very concerned to hear that school lunches may no longer be available. For school children, eating a good lunch can make all body functions run efficiently with enough energy to face the day's learning. In addition, school children are at a critical stage of growth and development, and the nutrition contained in lunch can provide necessary safeguard for physical development, so lunch is of great significance for students' physical growth and learning.

正文第一段中，作者对第一个要点进行了回复。作者在这里从两个方面，即：身体健康和学习说明了为什么午餐对学生如此重要。

School lunches can bring many benefits to parents and students. First, instead of preparing meals for students, parents can devote more energy to work or other things. Secondly, eating at school can reduce nutritional diseases such as malnutrition caused by nutritional deficiency and obesity caused by overnutrition, which is beneficial to correcting unhealthy eating habits of students such as picky eating, overeating and poor eating.

Finally, having the meal together also gives students the opportunity to sit down with their classmates, relax for about half an hour or so and have more time to communicate with classmates and teachers.

正文第二段是对第二个要点的回复，在这里作者从家长和学生两个方面说明了学校提供午餐带来的好处。对于家长来说，省去了准备午餐的麻烦，可以把更多的精力用在工作或其他事情上。对于学生来说，在学校吃午餐有利于纠正挑食、过度饮食、少食等不良饮食习惯，还可以有机会和同学、老师进行交流。

I don't think schools should cancel the lunch. Instead, they should provide healthier and cheaper meals for students. A wide variety of meals can provide students with comprehensive nutrition, such as salads, vegetables and fruits. Eating these healthy foods helps students avoid junk food. Schools can compare a number of food suppliers and choose one with the best quality and the lowest price. Schools can even grow vegetables in an area of the campus, which can not only save money, but also enable students to eat healthier food, and students can even participate in the planting and picking.

正文第三段是对第三个要点的回复，在这里作者详细说明了为什么需要让学校的膳食更便宜、更健康 "A wide variety of meals can provide students with comprehensive nutrition, such as salads, vegetables, and fruits. Eating these healthy foods helps students avoid junk food." 同时对如何提供更便宜、更健康的午餐提出了具体的措施，比如对多个菜品供应商进行比较、选择；在学校的空地上种植蔬菜等。

I really hope the school will reconsider this matter and be able to provide more nutritious food to the students.

最后一段是一个总结概况，表达了作者自己的愿望。

这篇范文中，作者对题目要求中的三个要点分别进行了回复，同时在对观点进行阐述的过程中，通过举例来进行说明，做到了有理有据，句子的表达也很流畅，是一篇很好的范文。

下面是完整的范文供参考：

I am very concerned to hear that school lunches may no longer be available. For school children, eating a good lunch can make all body functions run efficiently with enough energy to face the day's learning. In addition, school children are at a critical stage of growth and development, and the nutrition contained in lunch can provide necessary safeguard for physical development, so lunch is of great significance for students' physical growth and learning.

School lunches can bring many benefits to parents and students. First, instead of preparing meals for students, parents can devote more energy to work or other things. Secondly, eating at school can reduce nutritional diseases such as malnutrition caused by nutritional deficiency and obesity caused by overnutrition, which is beneficial to correcting unhealthy eating habits of students such as picky eating, overeating and poor eating. Finally, having the meal together also gives students the opportunity to sit down with their classmates, relax for about half an hour or so and have more time to communicate with classmates and teachers.

I don't think schools should cancel the lunch. Instead, they should provide healthier and cheaper meals for students. A wide variety of meals can provide students with comprehensive nutrition, such as salads, vegetables and fruits. Eating these healthy foods helps students avoid junk food. Schools can compare a number of food suppliers and choose one with the best quality and the lowest price. Schools can even grow vegetables in an area of the campus, which can not only save money, but also enable students to eat healthier food, and students can even participate in the planting and picking.

I really hope the school will reconsider this matter and be able to provide more nutritious food to the students.

范文翻译：

听说学校可能不再供应午餐了，这点令我很担心。对于上学的孩子来讲，午餐吃得好才能让身体各项机能高效运行，有充沛的精力面对一天的学习。此外，上学的孩子正处于生长发育的关键阶段，午餐提供的营养能为身体发育提供必要的保障，所以午餐对于学生的身体成长和学习都具有重要的意义。

学校提供午餐能为家长和学生带来很多益处。首先，家长不用再为学生准备午餐，可以把更多的精力用在工作或其他事情上。其次，在学校就餐可减少营养缺乏导致的营养不良、营养过剩导致的肥胖等营养性疾病，有利于纠正学生挑食、过度饮食、少食等不良饮食习惯。最后，一起吃午餐也让学生有机会和同学坐下来放松半个小时左右，有更多的时间跟同学和老师交流。

我认为学校不应该取消午餐，相反应该为学生提供更健康、便宜的饭菜。丰富的饭菜种类可以为学生提供全面的营养，比如沙拉、蔬菜和水果。食用这些健康的食物有助于学生避免垃圾食品。学校可以对多个菜品供应商进行比较，选择最质优价廉的供应商。学校甚至可以在校园的一个区域种植蔬菜，这样不仅可以节省费用，还可以让学生吃到更健康的食物，学生甚至还可以参与到种植和采摘的过程。

我真的希望学校能重新考虑这件事，并能够为学生提供更多有营养的食物。

➤重点词汇及短语

1. concerned [kən'sɜːnd] *adj.* 担心的；忧虑的

2. available [ə'veɪləbl] *adj.* 可用的，可获得的；有空的

3. efficiently [ɪ'fɪʃntlɪ] *adv.* 效率高地；有效地

4. energy ['enədʒi] *n.* 精力；力量

5. critical ['krɪtɪkl] *adj.* 极重要的；关键的；至关紧要的

6. safeguard ['seefˌgɑːd] *n.* 保护，保卫；防护措施

7. significance [sɪg'nɪfɪkəns] *n.* 重要性，意义

8. reduce [rɪ'djuːs] *vt.* 减少，缩小

9. nutritional [njuˈtrɪʃənl] *adj.* 营养的；滋养的

10. disease [dɪ'ziːz] *n.* 病；疾病

11. malnutrition [ˌmælnjuːˈtrɪʃn] *n.* 营养不良

12. obesity [əʊ'biːsɪti] *n.* 肥胖，过胖；肥胖症

13. cancle ['kænsl] *vt.* 取消；撤销；终止

14. comprehensive [ˌkɒmprɪ'hensɪv] *adj.* 全部的；所有的

15. salad ['sæləd] *n.* （生吃的）蔬菜沙拉

16. avoid [ə'vɔɪd] *vt.* 避免；防止

17. junk [dʒʌŋk] *n.* 垃圾；无价值的东西

18. campus ['kæmpəs] *n.* 校园，校区

19. a wide variety of 种种，多种多样

20. participate in 参加；参与

➤重点句型及例句

1. instead of doing sth. 代替做某事；而不是做某事

例：They played baseball instead of doing homework.

他们不做功课而去玩棒球。

2. devote... to... 把……用于……

例：I could only devote two hours a day to the work.

我一天只能在这个工作上花两个小时。

3. be beneficial to... 对……有益处的

例：It can be beneficial to share your feelings with someone you trust.

与你信任的人分享你的情感会是有益的。

4. communicate with sb. 与某人交流

　　例：Dolphins use sound to communicate with each other.

　　　　海豚用声音相互沟通。

5. provide sth. for... 为……提供某物

　　例：We are here to provide a service for the public.

　　　　我们来这里是为公众服务。

二、信件

（一）写作格式

　　信件与电子邮件这两种文体在结构与格式上非常相似，信件的风格更为正式，与电子邮件相比，信件的内容更为丰富，篇幅更长。下面是信件常见的两种格式。

　　英文信件常见的页面布局有左对齐和改良左对齐两种格式，考生可参考下面提供的两种格式，对英文信件的写作布局进行了解：

左对齐格式：

（Sender's name）	发件人姓名，可省略不写
Sender's address	发件人地址
Date: 写信日期	
Receiver's name	收件人姓名
Receiver's address	收件人地址
（subject）	写信目的或主题
Dear xxx,	对收件人的称呼
Body	信件的主体部分
Yours sincerely,	结束敬语
Signature	发件人手写签名
Name	发件人机打姓名
Position	发件人职务

改良左对齐格式：

（Sender's name）	发件人姓名，可省略不写
Sender's address	发件人地址

Date: 写信日期

Receiver's name	收件人姓名
Receiver's address	收件人地址
（subject）	写信目的或主题
Dear xxx,	对收件人的称呼
Body	信件的主体部分
Yours sincerely,	结束敬语
Signature	发件人手写签名
Name	发件人机打姓名
Position	发件人职务

领思写作考试中，第二部分的信件写作提供从"称呼"到"结束敬语"的全部格式和内容即可，不需要提供信头部分发件人姓名、地址等相关信息。

（二）常用表达

结合前面提到的内容可知，信件的结构主要分为开头段、主体段、结尾段三部分，这三部分所起的作用不同，常用到的表达如下：

开头段通常需要对写信目的进行说明，同时回应原始邮件中提到的问题，常用句式包括：

1. Thank you for your letter of/ dated...

2. With reference to your letter of...

3. Further to your offer letter of...

4. In reply to your inquiry of...

5. I am writing to tell you that...

6. I was pleased to hear from you...

7. I have received your letter just this moment and I am writing at once because...

8. I am sorry it has taken me a long time to reply to your last letter but...

9. I was very sorry to hear...

10. You will be very glad to hear that...

主体部分需要对题目中要求的三点任务分别进行陈述，根据不同的回信事由，需要用到不同的表达方式。除了下面列出的常用表达外，考生还可以参考第一部分电子邮件中列出的各种表达：

1. I am writing to enquire about...

2. I am writing to confirm that...

3. I am writing to apologize for/ about...

4. I am writing to inform you of... / that...

5. I am writing to complain about...

6. Unfortunately，we have been unable to...

7. I am sorry for any inconvenience this has caused.

8. I can assure you that we will...

9. I am not satisfied with...

10. I must therefore insist that...

11. I would like further information about...

结尾段中，可以表达出希望未来保持联系或者尽快收到对方回复的话语，常用的表达如下：

1. I would be very grateful if you could send me...

2. If you have any further questions/ queries, please（feel free to）contact me on（exact phone number）...

3. I look forward to hearing from you soon/ in due course/ in the near future.

4. I hope to hear from you soon.

5. Please write back soon.

6. I would appreciate it if you could send me...

7. Your kind and early reply will be appreciated.

8. I would appreciate it if you could give me a reply at your earliest convenience.

9. I hope that the above information will help you.

10. Please let me know if you need any further information.

11. We would appreciate it if you could...as soon as possible.

12. I'm expecting to hear from you as soon as possible.

（三）典型例题及详解

Your town council is thinking about banning the use of mobile phones on public transport and in shops and restaurants.

Write a letter to the town council.

Write about:

· your opinion about banning the use of mobile phones

· the reasons why you think it is a good idea or not

· the measures to take to ban the use of mobile phones in the public

and any other points you think are important.

Write at least 180 words.

观察上面的内容可以了解到，你所在的镇议会正在考虑禁止在公共交通、商店、餐馆使用手机。你需要给镇议会写一封信。

观察题目中的写作要求，三个小黑点分别代表三个要求，分别为你对禁止使用手机有何看法、说出你认为这是个好主意或不是好主意的原因以及有何措施禁止在公众场合使用手机。考生在写作的过程中可以根据任务要求来组织文章内容，同时需要注意，在写作的过程中需要对三点任务要求分别进行说明和陈述。

下面是一篇参考范文，一共包含五个段落。范文按照信件的格式对题目中的问题进行了相应回复。下面将对范文进行详细说明。

To whom it may concern,

I am writing to express my opinion on whether to ban mobile phones in public places, why we should do so, and the specific measures to ban them.

信件开头部分的称呼语使用的是"To whom it may concern"的表达，因为不知道收件人的姓名和性别，这种表达既能表达出尊敬，也不会有冒犯之意。

信件第一段对写作目的进行了概括说明，也是对题目中三点写作要求的改写。

Mobile phones have become an integral part of our daily lives, but they can be a nuisance when used in public places such as libraries and train stations. In my opinion, mobile phones should be banned in public places and this action will make public places more quiet and peaceful.

信件正文第二段是对第一个要点的回复。在这里作者表达了自己的观点"In my

opinion, mobile phones should be banned in public places and this action will make public places more quiet and peaceful." 即应该禁止在公共场所使用手机。

There are several downsides to using cell phones in public places. For one thing, the radiation from cell phones may have negative impacts on the bodies of users and those around them. Secondly, ringtones and talking on the phone can cause interference to people nearby. Finally, mobile phone theft has recently become a major crime in society as people use mobile phones in public places.

信件正文第三段是对第二个要点的回复。在这一段中作者分别从三个方面对原因进行了陈述，在这里作者使用了接续词For one thing, Secondly 和Finally，接续词的使用使文章层次更清晰，表达也更有逻辑。

As for banning cell phones in public places, the options are as follows: keeping the voice on the phone low on quiet public transport, violators will face a certain amount of fine; and if you have to use your phone, please do so outside or adjust it to the silent mode.

信件正文第四段是对第三个要点的回复。作者在这一段中对禁止在公共场所打电话的情况进行了说明，同时说明了如果需要打电话，应该如何处理。

I hope you will peruse my letter, and I shall be delighted if my thoughts come in handy.

Best wishes,

Jesson

信件最后部分是结束语、祝福语和发件人姓名。作者希望自己的信件被读到，提供的建议被采纳。并写上了祝福语和自己的姓名。

下面是完整的范文供参考：

To whom it may concern,

I am writing to express my opinion on whether to ban mobile phones in public places, why we should do so, and the specific measures to ban them.

Mobile phones have become an integral part of our daily lives, but they can be a nuisance when used in public places such as libraries and train stations. In my opinion, mobile phones should be banned in public places and this action will make public places more quiet and peaceful.

There are several downsides to using cell phones in public places. For one thing, the radiation from cell phones may have negative impacts on the bodies of users and people nearby. Secondly, ringtones and talking on the phone can cause interference to those around them. Finally, mobile phone theft has recently become a major crime in society as people use mobile phones in public places.

As for banning cell phones in public places, the options are as follows: keeping the voice on the phone low on quiet public transport, violators will face a certain amount of fine; and if you have to use your phone, please do so outside or adjust it to the silent mode.

I hope you will peruse my letter, and I shall be delighted if my thoughts come in handy.

Best wishes,
Jesson

范文翻译：

致相关人士：

我写这封信是想就是否在公共场所禁止（使用）手机、为什么我们应该这样做，以及禁止（使用）手机的具体措施表达我的意见。

手机已经成为我们日常生活中不可分割的一部分，但在图书馆和火车站等公共场所使用手机可能会令人讨厌。在我看来，在公共场所应该禁止使用手机，这将使公共场所更加安静、平和。

在公共场所使用手机有几个缺点。首先，手机辐射会对使用者和周围人的身体产生一些不良影响。其次，铃声和打电话会对周围的人造成干扰。最后，由于人们在公共场所使用手机，手机盗窃最近已成为社会上的一种主要犯罪行为。

关于在公共场所禁止使用手机，有以下几种选择：在安静的公共交通工具上不要使用手机大声说话，违者将面临一定数额的罚款；如果必须使用手机，请在室外使用或将手机调成静音模式。

我希望您能仔细阅读我的信，如果我的想法派上用场，我会很高兴的。

祝好，
杰森

➤ 重点词汇及短语

1. express [ɪkˈspres] *vt.* 表达，表示；不言自明

2. ban [bæn] *vt.* 禁止；取缔

3. specific [spəˈsɪfɪk] *adj.* 明确的；独特的

4. integral [ˈɪntɪgrəl] *adj.* 必需的；不可或缺的

5. nuisance [ˈnjuːsns] *n.* 麻烦事；讨厌的人（或东西）

6. library [ˈlaɪbrəri] *n.* 图书馆；藏书楼

7. peaceful [ˈpiːsfl] *adj.* 和平的；平和的；宁静的

8. downside [ˈdaʊnsaɪd] *n.* 下降趋势；负面，消极面

9. radiation [ˌreɪdiˈeɪʃn] *n.* 辐射；放射物；辐射状

10. ringtone [ˈrɪŋtəʊn] *n.* 手机铃音

11. interference [ˌɪntəˈfɪərəns] *n.* 干涉，干扰，冲突

12. theft [θeft] *n.* 偷窃，盗窃（罪）

13. crime [kraɪm] *n.* 罪行，犯罪活动

14. violator [ˈvaɪəleɪtə (r)] *n.* 违犯者

➤ 重点句型及例句

1. express opinion on... 发表关于……意见

例：Our responsibility is to express an opinion on these financial statements based on our audit.

我们的责任是在实施审计工作的基础上对财务报表发表意见。

三、帖子

（一）常用表达

英文帖子常常涉及对观点的表述及提出某种建议和意见，对观点进行表述常用到的句型在小短文部分已经列出了很多，考生可以参考记忆。这里将列出提出某种建议和意见的常用表达。

提供建议的常用句型

1. I think we should... 我认为我们应该……

2. I don't know if... is a good idea. 我不知道……是否是个好主意。

3. Maybe you should try... 也许你们应该试试……

4. My advice is to... 我的建议是……

5. I think the most suitable...for us is... 我认为对我们来说最适合的……是……

6. I would like to suggest that... 我想建议……

7. As far as I am concerned/ In my opinion, it would be wise to take the following action. 在我看来，采取如下行动是明智的。

8. I think it would be more beneficial if you could... 我认为如果你能……将会更有益。

9. There is no doubt that enough concern must be paid to the problem of... 毫无疑问，对……问题应予以足够的重视。

10. It must be realized that... 我们必须意识到……

（二）典型例题及详解

You have seen this announcement on your local government website:

> Is littering a problem in our town?
>
> It is clear that the amount of litter on our roads is increasing. We often get complaints from residents about all the rubbish that has piled up on the roads. We would like your suggestions for preventing people from littering in order to improve the environment for residents.
>
> Please let us know what you think and post your suggestions on our website.

Write your post for the local government website.

Write about:

• what has caused the increasing amount of litter in your town

• what problems the expanded littering is causing in your town

• how the amount of litter in your town could be reduced

and any other points you think are important.

Write at least 180 words.

　　观察上面的内容可以了解到，题目中提供的是当地政府网站发布的公告。公告的内容是关于乱扔垃圾的问题，由于街道上的垃圾数量不断增加，政府部门经常收到居民对堆积在街上的垃圾的投诉。政府网站想收集人们关于改善居民生活想法的文章。

公告下方是写作要求，首先对体裁进行了规定，"your post for the local government website" 可知需要写一篇帖子。接着是对写作内容的规定，分别为是什么造成了你所在城镇垃圾的数量在增加、随处乱扔垃圾的现象在你所在的城镇造成了什么问题以及如何减少城镇内的垃圾。考生在写作的过程中可以根据写作要求中提供的方向来组织文章内容。

下面是一篇参考范文，一共包含四个段落。分别从题目要求中的三个方面对观点进行了说明。

I am writing this post to address and make some suggestions regarding complaints about littering in our town.

帖子第一段是总起段，对整篇文章的写作目的进行了说明。

I think there are many reasons for the increasing number of rubbish in the town. First of all, with the development of express delivery and take-out, plastic products are abused, and disposable plastic products such as take-out lunch boxes and plastic bags are used to increase domestic rubbish. Secondly, commodities are overpackaged. Packing boxes and packaging materials are used in a heap, which is pompous without any preservation value. Finally, people are not aware of environmental protection and are lack of environmental protection education, so they throw garbage at will.

帖子正文第二段是对第一个写作要点的回复，在这里作者分析了垃圾数量增多的原因。作者从三个方面进行了说明，分别是快递和外卖行业带来的垃圾、商品过度包装带来的垃圾及人们薄弱的环保意识。

As we can see, littering has caused various kinds of problems in our town. In the first place, rubbish is everywhere in the streets, making the living environment of the whole town not comfortable. It will also affect the outcome of our city's application for civilized city. Secondly, the large amount of rubbish will do a lot of harm to the eco-system and people's life. Rubbish emits harmful greenhouse gases that damage the air and atmosphere. Rubbish also has a negative impact on wildlife, as animals may ingest inedible materials such as plastic bags, cans and bottles.

帖子正文第三段是对第二个写作要点的回复。对于随处乱扔垃圾产生的问题，作者从三个方面进行了说明，分别是街道上的垃圾影响人们的居住环境，同时影响文明城市的评选，其次垃圾会排放有害的温室气体，损害生态系统和大气，最后提到垃圾还会对野生动物产生负面影响。在对问题进行说明的过程中，作者使用了衔接词 In the first place，Secondly，Finally，使内容衔接更自然。

As for how to solve the problem of littering, I think we can start from two aspects: raising people's awareness of environmental protection and making relevant laws by local governments to prohibit littering. Many people are unaware of the dangers of littering, so through proper education, they will pay more attention to it in the future. In addition, the government has no laws to prohibit littering, and there are few penalties for littering. If the government imposed a fine every time someone litters in an open space, I think it would stop people from littering constantly.

帖子正文第四段是对第三个写作要点的回复。作者在这里讲到了如何减少城市内的垃圾，从两个方面入手，分别是"raising people's awareness of environmental protection"提高人们的意识；和"making relevant laws by local governments to prohibit littering"制定并执行更严格的反对乱扔垃圾的法律。

整篇文章结构严谨，逻辑清晰，是一篇非常好的范文。

下面是完整的范文供参考：

I am writing this post to address and make some suggestions regarding complaints about littering in our town.

I think there are many reasons for the increasing number of rubbish in the town. First of all, with the development of express delivery and take-out, plastic products are abused, and disposable plastic products such as take-out lunch boxes and plastic bags are used to increase domestic rubbish. Secondly, commodities are overpackaged. Packing boxes and packaging materials are used in a heap, which is pompous without any preservation value. Finally, people are not aware of environmental protection and are lack of environmental protection education, so they throw garbage at will.

As we can see, littering has caused various kinds of problems in our town. In the first place, rubbish is everywhere in the streets, making the living environment of the whole town not comfortable. It will also affect the outcome of our city's participation in the selection of civilized cities. Secondly, the large amount of rubbish will do a lot of harm to the ecosystem and people's life. Rubbish emits harmful greenhouse gases that damage the air and atmosphere. Finally, rubbish also has a negative impact on wildlife, as animals may ingest inedible materials such as plastic bags, cans and bottles.

As for how to solve the problem of littering, I think we can start from two aspects: raising people's awareness of environmental protection and making relevant laws by local governments to prohibit littering. Many people are unaware of the dangers of littering, so through proper education, they will pay more attention to it in the future. In addition, the government has no laws to prohibit littering, and there are few penalties for littering. If the government imposed a fine every time someone litters in an open space, I think it would stop people from littering.

范文翻译：

我写这篇帖子是就我们镇上关于乱扔垃圾的投诉提出一些建议。

我认为城镇垃圾增多有多方面的原因。首先随着快递和外卖的发展，塑料制品滥用，外卖餐盒和塑料袋等一次性塑料制品的使用使生活垃圾变多。其次，很多商品过度包装，包装盒和包装材料大肆使用，既华而不实也无保存价值。最后，人们环保意识不强，缺乏环保教育，垃圾随手扔。

我们可以发现，乱扔垃圾给我们镇上带来了各种各样的问题。首先，街道上的垃圾随处都是，使得整个城镇的居住环境不那么舒适。也会影响我们参加文明城市的评选。其次，大量的垃圾会给生态系统和人们的生活带来很多危害。垃圾会排放出有害的温室气体，损害空气和大气。最后垃圾还会对野生动物产生负面影响，因为动物可能会摄入不可食用的材料，如塑料袋、罐头盒和瓶子。

对于如何解决乱扔垃圾的问题，我认为可以从两方面来入手：提高人们的环保意识和地方政府制定相关的法律来禁止乱扔垃圾。许多人没有意识到乱扔垃圾的危害，所以通过适当的教育，他们将来会更加注意。此外，目前政府还没有相关的法律来禁止乱扔垃圾，对乱扔垃圾的处罚很少。如果每次有人在空地上丢弃垃圾，政府都会处以罚款，我认为这将阻止人们不断乱扔垃圾的行为。

➢ 重点词汇及短语

1. address [ə'dres] *vt.* 设法解决；处理；提出

2. complaint [kəm'pleɪnt] *n.* 抱怨；埋怨；投诉；控告

3. litter ['lɪtə (r)] *vt.* 乱扔

4. rubbish ['rʌbɪʃ] *n.* 垃圾；废弃物

5. plastic ['plæstɪk] *adj.* 塑料制的；塑料的

6. abuse [ə'bjuːz] *vt.* 滥用；妄用

7. disposable [dɪ'spəuzəbl] *adj.* 用后即丢弃的；一次性的

8. pompous ['pɒmpəs] *adj.* 浮华的，华而不实的

9. comfortable ['kʌmftəbl] *adj.* 使人舒服的；舒适的

10. civilized ['sɪvəlaɪzd] *adj.* 文明的；开化的

11. ecosystem ['iːkəusɪstəm] *n.* 生态系统

12. emit [i'mɪt] *vt.* 发出，射出，散发（光、热、声音、气等）

13. harmful ['hɑːmfl] *adj.* （尤指对健康或环境）有害的，导致损害的

14. greenhouse ['griːnhaus] *n.* 温室；暖房

15. negative ['negətɪv] *adj.* 坏的；有害的

16. wildlife ['waɪldlaɪf] *n.* 野生动物；野生生物

17. ingest [ɪn'dʒest] *vt.* 摄入；食入；咽下

18. inedible [ɪn'edəbl] *adj.* 不能吃的；不宜食用的

19. prohibit [prə'hɪbɪt] *vt.* （尤指以法令）禁止

20. penalty ['penəlti] *n.* 惩罚；处罚；刑罚

21. impose [ɪm'pəuz] *vt.* 推行，采用（规章制度）；强制实行

22. express delivery 快递

23. overpackaged 过度包装的

24. in a heap 成山，成堆，累累

➢ 重点句型及例句

1. make some suggestions 提出一些建议

　　例：Can you make some suggestions as for what I should do?

　　　　你能就我该做些什么提些建议吗?

2. have an impact on... 对于……有影响；对……造成冲击

　　例：The medication didn't have an impact on the patient's illness.

　　　　药物治疗对这个病人毫无效果。

3. stop sb. from doing... 阻止某人做……

　　例：It may even stop them from doing something stupid.

　　　　这甚至可以阻止他们做一些愚蠢的事情。

四、常用功能表达句

（一）表达必要性

- Construction should be finished by... 工程应该在……之前完成。
- We definitely need to get better at.... 我们确实需要更好地……
- We need to get... 我们需要得到……
- What kind of... will we have to deal with? 我们要面对什么样的……？
- You must inform... 您必须通知……
- Your monthly supply budget should not exceed... 你们每月的供应预算不应超过……
- You don't have to wear a suit. It's an informal occasion. 您用不着穿正装，这是一个非正式场合。

（二）强调重要性

- It's important to... 重要的是要……
- One of the first things we've got to do is... 我们首先要做的一件事情就是……
- That's where we need to... 那正是我们需要……的。
- The best thing about this product is that it... 这个产品最好的一点是它……
- The first thing we will need is... 我们首先需要的是……
- Be sure to put down the address of the receiver clearly. 注意要把收件人的地址写清楚。
- Make sure you check all the equipment. 一定要检查所有的设备。
- Make sure it doesn't happen again. 下不为例。

（三）做比较

同样

- ... just as well as... ……和……一样好。
- I earn the same as I did... ago. 我和……之前挣得一样多。

- I'm not as busy now as I was... 我现在没有……忙。

- We don't sell as much as we used to. 我们没有过去卖得多。

- We're as big as our main competitor. 我们和我们的主要竞争对手规模一样大。

更加

- I think my arguments were more persuasive than... 我觉得我的观点比……更有说服力。

- She's much more... than her colleagues. 她比她的同事们更……

- We have fewer students than we used to have. 我们的学生比过去少了。

- You're more experienced in these matters than I am. 您在这些事情上比我更有经验。

不一样

- It will run much more efficiently if we get it serviced. 这个如果拿去修修会运转得更好。

- It will take much less time if we send it by express delivery. 用快递寄会快得多。

- We sold slightly more this year than last year. 我们今年比去年卖得多一点。

- The weather of this year is not the same as that of the past years. 今年的气候同往年不一样。

（四）比较数据

- It's the... most expensive city in the world. 这是排在全球第……的生活最昂贵的城市。

- It's the... largest pharmaceutical company in... 这是……第……大的制药公司。

- She earns half as much as he does. 她的收入是他的一半。

- The new warehouse is almost... as big as the old one. 新库房是旧库房的……倍大。

- Their advertising budget is... times as much as ours. 他们的广告预算是我们的……倍。

- They spend... as much on raw materials as we do. 他们在原材料上的支出是我们的……倍。

（五）说明数量

- Could you call the restaurant and make a reservation for... people? 你能打电话给

那家餐厅预订……人的座位吗?.

- His new laptop is only... inches thick. 他的新笔记本电脑厚度仅为……英寸。

- I spend about... hours every day writing e-mails. 我每天花……小时左右写电子邮件。

- Over... people have signed up for the conference. 本次会议共有……多人报名参加。

- Please bring... copies of the handout to the conference. 请带……份讲义的复印件来开会。

- The author's latest book is roughly... pages long. 这个作家的新书大约有……页。

- The company has over... employees worldwide. 这家公司在全球有……多名员工。

(六) 说明数字

面积

- My garden is about... feet long and... feet wide. 我的花园长约……英尺，宽约……英尺。

- The Central Park covers an area of... square meters. 中央公园的占地面积是……平方米。

- The floor area is only around... square feet. 楼层总面积只有大约……平方英尺。

- The new golf resort covers more than... acres of land. 新高尔夫球场的占地面积是……多英亩。

倍数和百分比

- Did you hear that the unemployment rate has dropped to below...? 您听说了吗？失业率已经下降到……以下了。

- He decided to invest... percent of his savings in the stock market. 他决定把自己存款的百分之……投资到股市中。

- Her new house is about ... times bigger than her old one. 她的新房子比旧房子大了约……倍。

- His fortune has increased more than... in the past... months. 在过去……个月里，他的财富暴增……倍多。

- Our company's earnings rose by... this quarter. 这个季度我们公司的盈利增加了……

- Our... market share has dropped... over the past year. 去年一年我们在……的市

场占有率下降了⋯⋯

- The price of oil has... in less than... years. 不到⋯⋯年，石油的价格⋯⋯。

比例

- Last month, approximately... of all transactions were made through our website-an increase of... from a year ago. 上个月我们网站的交易额接近总交易额的⋯⋯，比去年增长了⋯⋯

- Online purchases accounted for some... of last month's sales revenues. 上个月的在线购物营业额已达到总销售额的⋯⋯

- What proportion of your income do you spend on food? 您在食品上的花费占收入的比例是多少？

平均值

- ... said he has an average grade of about... ⋯⋯说他的平均分大概是⋯⋯

- I get an average of ... hours of sleep per night. 我平均每晚睡⋯⋯小时。

- The average annual temperature here is... degrees Celsius. 这里的年平均气温是⋯⋯摄氏度。

- The average lifespan has risen in the past... years. 在过去的⋯⋯年间，平均寿命有所增加。

- The average precipitation in April is... millimeters. 4月的平均降水量是⋯⋯毫米。

- The report shows our average daily sales were... 报告显示，我们的日均销售额达到了⋯⋯

Day 8　实战篇

1.

You should spend about 30 minutes on this task.

Your college has a website where students can write reviews of places they have visited and activities they have done. You have recently seen a film and decided to write a review on the website.

In your film review, you should:

· include a description of the film

· give your own opinion of the film

· state whether you would recommend the film to other people and any other points you think are important.

Write at least 180 words.

2.

You should spend about 30 minutes on this task.

You work in a city council and you have been asked to warn the local population about a possible heat wave in the next few days.

Write an email to your inhabitants to:

· let them know about a possible heat wave

· tell them what recommendations to follow

· ask them to share your email with other people

and any other points you think are important.

Write at least 180 words.

3.

You should spend about 30 minutes on this task.

You have seen this competition organized by an online travel magazine.

Do you want to be a travel writer? All you have to do is to write an article for our website, based on a personal travel experience.

The title of the article should be "My Best Journey".

Upload your article to our competition page.

Write the article for the online travel magazine.

Write about:

• where you went on your best journey

• why the journey was special for you

• whether you would recommend the journey to everyone

and any other points you think are important.

Write at least 180 words.

4.

You should spend about 30 minutes on this task.

Your school magazine is going to publish a special edition to welcome students back to school for the new school year. You have been asked to write an article about the importance of setting study goals.

In your article you should explain:

• the importance of setting study goals

• what type of goals students should set

• where students can find the support they need to achieve their goals

and any other points which you think are important.

Write at least 180 words.

考前冲刺——全真模拟题

Day 9 考前冲刺篇

全真模拟题一

Part 1

You should spend about 15 minutes on this task.

Your dog is missing. You wish to inform all your neighbors.

Send them an email and in your email you should:

• explain the situation

• describe the dog

• tell them what they can do to help.

Write at least 50 words.

Part 2

You should spend about 30 minutes on this task.

You have seen this notice on your college website.

Write us a review of a website that you have used for studying!

Tell us about a website that you have used for studying. What is good about it? Could it be improved? Who would you recommend the website to?

Write a review of a website that you have used for studying.

Write about:

• why you like the website

• what could make the website better

• who you would recommend the website to

and any other points which you think are important.

Write at least 180 words.

Part 1

You should spend about 15 minutes on this task.

You have received this email from an online shop you have bought something from.

Dear customer,

Thank you for your order.

Our delivery driver will contact you when he's near.

You said that the best time for the delivery was in the morning. We know people are busy, so can you tell us a place for the driver to leave the package if you are out?

Best wishes,

Kelly

Sales team

Write an email to Kelly, and you should:

• say when you will be available to receive the delivery in the morning

• describe where the delivery driver can leave the package if you are out

• explain the best way for the delivery driver to contact you.

Write at least 50 words.

Part 2

You should spend about 30 minutes on this task.

The town where you live has a website where you can discuss local issues. You recently visited a new leisure centre which is advertised below.

Write a review for the website.

In your review mention:

• transport/ access to the centre

- equipment and facilities
- what kind of people the leisure center suits

and any other points you think are important.

Write at least 180 words.

Ivy Vine Leisure Centre

Welcome to our modern leisure center for a free experience. It is conveniently located less than a mile from the city centre.

Here you can experience the latest fitness equipment and skate in our Olympic-sized skating rink. If you're hungry after exercising, no problem, our cafes and restaurants serve a wide range of flavors. The leisure center staff are experienced and can answer all your health questions.

参考范文与翻译

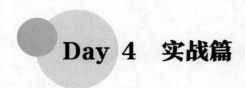

Day 4 实战篇

1.

题目翻译：

你收到了你的朋友雷纳德发来的邮件：

发件人：雷纳德

　　你好！我下周要去你所在的城市度假。我正考虑住在离市中心近一点的地方，但我不太确定。你知道我在这期间能做些什么吗？如果你有空，我们可以见个面。

雷纳德

给你的朋友雷纳德写一封电子邮件：

- 说明你认为你的朋友应该住在哪里
- 为你的朋友推荐一些可以做的事情
- 建议一个时间跟朋友见面

至少写50个单词。

参考范文：

Hi Leonard,

It's great to hear from you. How have you been?

I think you should definitely stay near the city centre because it would be more convenient for you. There are many shops and restaurants in this area. In addition, you would be able to reach other parts of the city easily since all the subway and bus lines run through the city centre.

I would suggest that you visit the city's attractions when you're here. There are lots of renowned museums and ancient buildings, and there's even an amusement park. If you need a break from everything, you could either relax at a park or take a train to the outskirts of the city where it's more peaceful and quiet.

We should definitely meet up while you're here! I'll be busy from Monday to Thursday because of a work deadline, but I'll be free after that. Perhaps we could have dinner on Friday night or I could take you to some places during the weekend. Just let me know what works best for you.

Can't wait to see you soon!

Your friend,
Andrew

范文翻译：

嗨，雷纳德：

很高兴收到你的来信。你最近怎么样？

我认为你绝对应该住在市中心附近，因为那里对你来说更方便。这个地区有许多商店和餐馆。此外，你可以很容易地到达城市的其他地方，因为所有的地铁和公交线路都经过市中心。

我建议你在这里的时候去参观一下这个城市的景点。这里有很多著名的博物馆和古建筑，还有一个游乐园。如果你需要休息一下，你可以去公园放松一下，或者乘火车去市郊，那里更安静。

你来的时候我们一定要见个面！由于工作上的时间期限要求，我周一到周四会很忙，但那之后我就有空了。也许我们可以周五晚上一起吃晚饭，或者周末我带你去一些地方。只要告诉我什么最适合你就好。

等不及要见到你了！

你的朋友，
安德鲁

➤ 重点词汇及短语

1. entirely [ɪnˈtaɪəli] *adv.* 全部地；彻底地

2. definitely [ˈdefɪnətli] *adv.* 确切地；明确地

3. restaurant [ˈrestrɒnt] *n.* 餐馆；餐厅

4. subway [ˈsʌbweɪ] *n.* 地铁

5. attraction [əˈtrækʃn] *n.* 向往的地方；有吸引力的事；景点

6. renowned [rɪˈnaʊnd] *adj.* 有名的；闻名的；受尊敬的

7. ancient [ˈeɪnʃənt] *adj.* 古代的；古老的

8. amusement [əˈmjuːzmənt] *n.* 娱乐活动

9. outskirts [ˈaʊtskɜːts] *n.* （市镇的）边缘地带；市郊

10. peaceful [ˈpiːsfl] *adj.* 安静的；平静的

11. deadline [ˈdedlaɪn] *n.* 最后期限；截止日期

12. meet up（按照安排）见面，会面

➤ 重点句型及例句

1. consider doing... **考虑做……**

　　例：Why not consider doing it in a different way?

　　　　为什么不考虑用别的方法做呢？

2. hear from sb. **收到……的来信**

　　例：I hear from my mother every month.

　　　　我每月都收到我母亲的信。

3. be convenient for **方便……；便于……**

　　例：It's more convenient for modern people to live in a rapid way.

　　　　对现代人来说，快速的生活方式更方便。

2.

题目翻译：

和你的班级一起旅行

上周你和你班上的一些学生去旅行了。

给你的朋友约瑟夫写一封电子邮件，在您的电子邮件中：

· 说明你们去了哪里

· 说明你们做了什么

· 说说你为什么喜欢这次旅行。

至少写50个单词。

参考范文：

Dear Joseph,

I haven't seen you for a long time. Let me tell you something interesting.

Last week, I organized several of my students to go to a farm in the suburbs. We met at the school gate in the morning and arrived at our destination after an hour's bus ride. The farm staff welcomed us warmly and the farmer showed us around and taught us how to milk cows and mow grass. How refreshing it is to see the blue sky and the green grass! At noon, we had a picnic in the sunshine. After a short rest, we sang and danced merrily.

But the time passed quickly. Before we knew it, we had to say goodbye to the farm owner and the staff.

I wish I could have a trip like this again.

Have you traveled anywhere recently? Looking forward to you reply.

Best wishes for you!

Your friend,
Jefferson

范文翻译：

亲爱的约瑟夫：

我好久没见到你了。让我告诉你一件有趣的事情。

上周，我组织了几个学生去郊区的一个农场。我们早上在学校门口见面，坐了一个小时的公交车到达目的地。农场工作人员热情地欢迎我们，农民带我们四处参观，并教我们如何挤牛奶和割草。看到蓝天和绿草是多么令人心旷神怡啊！中午，我们在阳光下野餐。休息片刻后，我们欢快地载歌载舞。

但是时间过得很快。不知不觉中，我们不得不和农场主和工作人员说再见。

我希望能再有一次这样的旅行。

你最近去过什么地方吗？期待你的回复。

祝好！

你的朋友，
杰斐逊

➤ 重点词汇及短语

1. trip [trɪp] *vt.* 旅游，旅行

2. organize [ˈɔːɡənaɪz] *vt.* 组织；筹备；安排；组建

3. suburb [ˈsʌbɜːb] *n.* 郊区；城外

4. gate [ɡeɪt] *n.* 大门；栅栏门；围墙门

5. destination [ˌdestɪˈneɪʃn] *n.* 目的地；终点

6. warmly [wɔːmlɪ] *adv.* 温暖地；亲切地；热烈地；热心地

7. milk [mɪlk] *vt.* 挤奶

8. cow [kaʊ] *n.* 奶牛，母牛

9. mow [məʊ] *vt.* 割；修剪

10. refreshing [rɪˈfreʃɪŋ] *adj.* 使人精力充沛的；使人凉爽的

11. picnic [ˈpɪknɪk] *n.* 野餐

12. sunshine [ˈsʌnʃaɪn] *n.* 阳光；日光

13. merrily [ˈmerəli] *adv.* 快乐地，愉快地，兴高采烈地

➤ 重点句型及例句

1. show sb. around 带某人参观……

例：Only a skeleton staff remains to show anyone interested around the site.

只有极少数的员工留下来带领感兴趣的人参观场地。

2. how+adj. it is to do sth. 做某事多么……

例：How wonderful it is to go to Paris tomorrow!

明天去巴黎真是太好了！

3.

题目翻译：

你收到了餐厅经理发来的电子邮件：

发件人：理查德先生

希望您和您的朋友上一次在我们餐厅用餐愉快。你们走后，我们在你们坐的桌子下面发现了一条围巾和一副手套。这些东西是您的，还是您朋友的？

理查德先生（经理）

给理查德先生写一封电子邮件：

- 向经理表达你对餐厅的看法
- 解释围巾和手套属于谁
- 说明你们什么时候可以来领取物品

至少写50个单词。

参考范文：

Dear Mr. Richard,

Very glad to receive your email!

We like your restaurant very much. We had a long journey from the United States, and we arrived at the airport very tiredly. Thanks to your restaurant's special pickup service, which spared us the hassle of a cab ride, we had a nice rest in the car. Arriving at the restaurant, we got a good taste of home. The food is really good and your service is polite and comfortable.

The scarf left in your restaurant was my friend's. She missed it when we finished our meal. And the pair of gloves was a present for my daughter. I found it lost when I got home.

I will have the scarf and gloves back by Friday evening. Is it convenient for you? If it is not convenient, can I come to your restaurant at a fixed time when it is available?

I look forward to your reply and thank you again.

Best wishes!
Jane

范文翻译：

亲爱的理查德先生：

很高兴收到你的邮件！

我们非常喜欢你们的餐厅。我们从美国而来经历了很长的旅途，到达机场时非常疲惫。感谢贵餐厅的特殊接机服务，免去了打车的麻烦，我们在车里休息得很好。到了餐厅，我们尝到了家乡的味道。食物真的很美味，你们的服务很有礼貌，让人很舒服。

落在餐厅里的围巾是我朋友的。我们吃完饭的时候她落下了。那副手套是给我女儿的礼物。我回家时发现它丢了。

我会在星期五晚上把围巾和手套拿回来。你方便吗？如果不方便，我可以在你们餐厅有空的时候来取吗？

期待您的回复，再次表示感谢。

祝好！
简

➢ 重点词汇及短语

1. scarf [skɑːf] *n.* 围巾；头巾

2. glove [glʌv] *n.* 手套；棒球手套

3. journey [ˈdʒɜːni] *n.* （尤指长途）旅行，行程

4. tiredly [ˈtaɪədlɪ] *adv.* 疲劳地；累地；疲倦地

5. special [ˈspeʃl] *adj.* 特殊的；特别的

6. pickup [ˈpɪkʌp] *n.* 接人；收取物品

7. hassle [ˈhæsl] *n.* 困难；麻烦

8. polite [pəˈlaɪt] *adj.* 有礼貌的；客气的；儒雅的

9. comfortable [ˈkʌmftəbl] *adj.* 使人舒服的；舒适的

10. convenient [kənˈviːniənt] *adj.* 实用的；便利的；方便的；省事的

11. available [əˈveɪləbl] *adj.* 可获得的；可购得的；可找到的

➢ 重点句型及例句

1. thanks to…由于……，幸亏……

例：Thanks to the automobile, Americans soon had a freedom of movement previously unknown.

由于有了汽车，美国人很快就获得了前所未有的行动自由。

4.

题目翻译：

你收到了一位大学朋友发来的邮件：

你知道我跟你说过我想健身。嗯，我刚加入了你所在的那个运动中心。我想知道你是否可以推荐一些好的课程让我参加。你能告诉我什么时间去运动中心最好吗？我不想在人多的时候去。如果我们能找个时间一起上一堂课，或者喝杯咖啡，那就太好了。

有时间给我发邮件。

威廉

给威廉写一封电子邮件：

• 向他推荐一些运动中心的课程

• 说明什么时间去运动中心最好

- 邀请威廉在运动中心的咖啡馆见面

至少写50个单词。

参考范文：

Hi William,

It's good to hear from you. I'm so glad you've joined in my gym.

I think you should try the beginners' spin classes. It's not too challenging and fun. And I'd recommend the Pilates classes. You've done Pilates before, haven't you?

I think a lot of people go to the centre after work, which means most classes get booked up in the early evening. So, it's best to go during the day or after 8 p.m.

I tend to go for a swim in the early morning at the weekend, so do you fancy meeting up for a swim or sauna?

Good luck with your fitness plan and I hope we can get together sometime soon.

Take care,

Jenny

范文翻译：

你好威廉：

很高兴收到你的来信。我很高兴你加入了我所在的那家健身房。

我觉得你应该试试初级的动感单车课。它不是太有挑战性，而且很有趣。我推荐普拉提课程。你以前做过普拉提，对吧？

我觉得很多人下班后都会去这个运动中心，这也就意味着大多数傍晚的课程已经订满了。所以，最好在白天或晚上8点以后去。

我常常在周末清晨去游泳，所以你想和我一起去游泳或蒸桑拿吗？

祝你健身计划顺利，希望我们很快能聚在一起。

多保重！
詹妮

➤ **重点词汇及短语**

1. gym [dʒɪm] *n.* 健身房；体育馆
2. challenging [ˈtʃælɪndʒɪŋ] *adj.* 挑战性的；考验能力的
3. recommend [ˌrekəˈmend] *vt.* 推荐；举荐；介绍
4. Pilates [pɪˈlɑːtiz] *n.* 普拉提，一种健身体操
5. sauna [ˈsɔːnə] *n.* 桑拿浴；蒸汽浴
6. get fit 健身；塑形；让身体变健康

➤ **重点句型**

1. I wonder if... 不知是否可以……；我想知道是否……

    例：I wonder if you'd be kind enough to give us some information, please?
    不知能否请您向我们提供些信息？

2. it would be great if... 如果……那就太好了

    例：It would be great if you could always jump straight to the high-tech solution, as you can with mobile phones.

如果你总是能直接找到高科技的解决方案，就像在手机行业那样，那就太好了。

3. tend to do…倾向于做某事

例：You'll tend to do the same activity for the rest of the day.

你往往会在一天中剩下的时间里做同样的事情。

4. fancy doing sth. 喜欢做某事

例：Do you fancy going out this evening?

今晚你想不想出去？

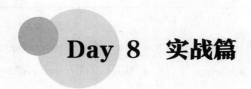

Day 8　实战篇

1.

题目翻译：

你应该在这项任务上花费大约30分钟。

你所在的学院有一个网站，学生们可以在这个网站上写下他们对去过的地方和他们所做过的活动的评论。你最近看了一部电影，决定在网站上写一篇评论。

在你的影评中：
- 包括对这部影片的描述
- 给出你自己对影片的看法
- 说明你是否会向其他人推荐这部电影
以及其他你认为重要的点。

至少写180个单词。

参考范文：

Introduction

Whiplash is director Damien Chazelle's latest film. It's a psychological drama and it's set in a New York music academy. It stars Miles Teller who plays the character of Andy, an ambitious young jazz drummer.

Film Story

The film tells a moving story of Andy, who has been playing the drums since childhood and is determined to become a top jazz musician. He is noticed by teacher Terence Fletcher, played by J.K. Simmons, who sees Andy's talent and invites him to join his competitive jazz band. Fletcher bullies the band members, including Andy, and pushes them to achieve the impossible. Andy at first rises to the challenge of his teacher's demands, but as the film goes on, he becomes more and more exhausted and emotional.

Good and Bad Aspects

For me, the best aspect of the film was the unpredictable plot and the development of Andy's relationship with his teacher. The extended sections of musical performance were amazing, too. My only criticism was that I thought the film's central message was old-fashioned. The message was that in order to be perfect you have to suffer. However, it made me think and it challenged my ideas.

Recommendation

Whiplash is not to be missed. It's a gripping film with complex characters, and if you like jazz, you'll love the soundtrack.

范文翻译：

简介

《爆裂鼓手》是达米恩·查泽雷导演的最新电影。这是一部心理剧，以纽约的一所音乐学院为背景。这部电影由迈尔斯·特勒主演，他扮演安迪，一个雄心勃勃的年轻爵士乐鼓手。

电影情节

这部电影讲述了安迪的感人故事，他从小就打鼓，并决心成为一名顶级爵士音乐家。由 J.K 西蒙斯扮演的老师特伦斯·弗莱彻注意到了他，看到了安迪的才华，并邀请他加入他的充满竞争的爵士乐队。弗莱彻压榨包括安迪在内的乐队成员，并强迫他们完成不可能的事情。安迪起初接受老师要求的挑战，但随着电影的进行，他变得越来越疲惫和情绪化。

好的和坏的方面

对我来说，这部电影最好的方面是不可预测的情节和安迪与老师关系的发展。音乐表演的延伸部分也令人惊叹。我唯一不满的是，我认为这部电影的核心信息是过时的。它传达的信息是，为了完美，你必须受苦。然而，它让我思考，也挑战了我的观念。

建议

《爆裂鼓手》不容错过。这是一部扣人心弦的电影，人物复杂，如果你喜欢爵士乐，你会喜欢它的电影配乐。

> ➤ 重点词汇及短语

---

1. director [dəˈrektə(r)] *n.* （电影、戏剧等的）导演

2. latest [ˈleɪtɪst] *adj.* 最近的；最新的

3. psychological [ˌsaɪkəˈlɒdʒɪkl] *adj.* 心理的；精神上的；心理学的

4. drama [ˈdrɑːmə] *n.* 戏；剧

5. academy [əˈkædəmi] *n.* 专科院校

6. character [ˈkærəktə(r)] *n.* （书籍、戏剧或电影中的）人物，角色

7. ambitious [æmˈbɪʃəs] *adj.* 有野心的，有雄心的

8. jazz [dʒæz] *n.* 爵士乐

9. drummer [ˈdrʌmə(r)] *n.* 鼓手

10. childhood [ˈtʃaɪldhʊd] *n.* 童年；幼年；孩童时期

11. musician [mjuˈzɪʃn] *n.* 音乐家

12. talent [ˈtælənt] *n.* 天才；天资；天赋

13. competitive [kəmˈpetətɪv] *adj.* 竞争的

14. bully [ˈbʊli] *vt.* 恐吓；伤害；胁迫

15. achieve [əˈtʃiːv] *vt.* 实现，达到；完成

16. exhausted [ɪɡˈzɔːstɪd] *adj.* 筋疲力尽的；疲惫不堪的

17. emotional [ɪˈməʊʃənl] *adj.* 感情的；情感的；情绪的

18. unpredictable [ˌʌnprɪˈdɪktəbl] *adj.* 无法预言的；不可预测的

19. plot [plɒt] *n.* 故事情节；布局

20. amazing [əˈmeɪzɪŋ] *adj.* 令人大为惊奇的；（尤指）令人惊喜（或惊羡、惊叹）的

21. suffer [ˈsʌfə(r)] *vt.* 受苦；忍受；变差

22. complex [ˈkɒmpleks] *adj.* 复杂的；复合的

23. soundtrack [ˈsaʊndtræk] *n.* （电影的）声迹，声带

> ➤ 重点句型

1. be determined to... 坚决；下决心做……

   例：He is determined to win at any cost.

   他决心无论如何要争取胜利。

2. invite sb. to do sth. 邀请某人做某事

   例：My father and mother want to invite you to the movies.

   我爸爸妈妈想邀请你去看电影。

2.

题目翻译：

你应该在这项任务上花费大约30分钟。

你在市议会工作，你被要求提醒当地居民未来几天可能出现热浪。

写一封电子邮件给当地的居民：

- 告知他们可能会有热浪
- 告诉他们应该遵循哪些建议
- 让他们把你的电子邮件分享给其他人

以及其他你认为重要的点。

至少写180个单词。

参考范文：

Dear fellow citizens,

We have all suffered these past few days from unusual high temperatures. We believe that they may reach new peaks soon and a 3-day heat wave is quite likely according to weather forecast specialists.

It is essential to stay indoors as much as you can, to close your windows and curtains and to stop physical activities. It is also important to drink more water than usual, especially if you are a senior citizen or if you have young kids. We strongly recommend that you avoid sunbathing or outdoor activities especially from 10 a.m. to 5 p.m.. If you have an air conditioner at home, we encourage you to use it. Please note watering plants and garden during the day is now strictly prohibited and so is car washing.

To help us reach as many citizens as possible, we would like to invite you to forward this email to your family, friends and colleagues. You can also post the text on social media.

You can call us if you need any additional information.

Thank you for your help.

City Hall

范文翻译：

亲爱的市民们：

在过去的几天里，我们都遭受了罕见高温的折磨。根据天气预报专家的说法，气温很快就会达到新的峰值，而且很可能会出现一场为期3天的热浪。

大家必须尽可能多待在室内，关上窗户，拉上窗帘，停止体育活动。比平时多喝水也很重要，特别是如果您是老年人或者您有年幼的孩子，我们强烈建议您避免日光浴或户外活动，特别是在上午10点至下午5点之间。如果您家里有空调，我们鼓励你使用。请注意，现在严禁在白天浇灌植物和花园，禁止洗车。

为了帮助我们通知到尽可能多的公民，我们恳请您将此电子邮件转发给您的家人、朋友和同事。你也可以在社交媒体上发布这条信息。

如果你需要其他信息，可以打电话给我们。

谢谢你的帮助。

市政厅

➤ 重点词汇及短语

1. suffer ['sʌfə(r)] *vt/vi.* 受苦；忍受

2. unusual [ʌn'juːʒuəl] *adj.* 特别的；不寻常的；罕见的

3. temperature ['temprətʃə(r)] *n.* 温度；气温

4. peak [piːk] *n.* 顶峰；高峰

5. indoor ['ɪndɔː(r)] *adj.*（在）室内的；在户内进行的

6. curtain ['kɜːtn] *n.* 窗帘

7. stop [stop] *vt.* 停止；结束

8. recommend [ˌrekə'mend] *vt.* 劝告；建议

9. sunbathe ['sʌnbeɪð] *vi.* 沐日光浴

10. prohibit [prə'hɪbɪt] *vt.* 禁止；阻止

11. forward ['fɔːwəd] *vt.* 发送，寄（商品或信息）

12. heat wave 热浪

13. according to 据（……所说）；按（……所报道）

14. senior citizen 老年人

15. social media 社交媒体

➤ 重点句型

1. it is essential to do sth. 至关重要的是……

    例：To promote bilateral cooperation，it is essential to enhance mutual understand-
    ing.

    为了促进双方的合作，必须加强彼此的了解.

2. avoid doing sth. 避免做某事

    例：If you avoid doing the following things you will be off to a good start as you
    make this transition.

    避免去做下面这些事，你就能很好地完成这个转变，并且拥有一个良好的
    开端。

3. encourage sb. to do sth. 鼓励某人做某事

    例：We encourage all members to strive for the highest standards.
    我们鼓励所有成员为达到最高标准而努力。

3.

题目翻译：

你应该在这项任务上花费大约30分钟。

你看到了这个由一家在线旅游杂志组织的比赛。

你想成为一名游记作家吗？你只需要根据个人旅行经验为我们的网站写一篇文章。

文章的标题应为"我的最佳旅程"。

将您的文章上传到我们的竞赛页面。

为在线旅游杂志写一篇文章。
文章内容包括：
- 你在哪里度过了最美好的旅程
- 为什么这次旅行对你来说很特别
- 你是否会向所有人推荐这次旅行
以及其他你认为重要的点。

至少写180个单词。

参考范文：

In this article I will explain my particular journey to America, and the special experiences I gained on that journey.

About ten years ago, I worked as a camp organizer and took three kids to the US for a summer camp organized by a local elementary school. It was my first time on a plane to the United States and my first time caring for three 8-year-old girls.

I was a bit nervous before the trip, not knowing what to expect on the plane. As the plane flew along, everything seemed fine, and the girls enjoyed the delicious food the plane provided and the excitement of being in another country. After one or two hours' travel, the girls were a little exhausted and we had to spend about twelve hours on the plane. I talked to them and suggested that they should go to the toilet and move their bodies. As the night wore on, they grew drowsy. I got help from the airline stewardess to put them in warm blankets. After a good night's sleep they were better, and expected to see the camp school in another country.

When we arrived at the local American elementary school, we were greeted warmly by the organizers, and the kids were curious about life in a different country. As I watched the excitement on their faces, I felt that the hard work in caring for them had been well worth it.

At the same time, I had the opportunity to experience the different cultures between China and the United States. More importantly, I gained the experience of caring for children, which is very important for a teacher or a mother.

That trip was my first visit to the United States. I've visited some of the sights of America, like the Statue of Liberty, and I've been to the cities of New York and Philadelphia. I would like to recommend this journey to everyone as it was really a great experience.

范文翻译：

在这篇文章中，我将叙述我的美国之旅，以及我在这段旅程中收获的独特经历。

大约十年前，我作为一名夏令营组织者，带着三个孩子去美国参加了当地一所小学组织的夏令营。这是我第一次坐飞机去美国，也是我第一次照顾三个8岁的女孩。

旅行前我有点紧张，不知道飞机上会发生什么。飞机飞行的时候，一切似乎都很好，女孩们享受着飞机提供的美味食物以及来到另一个国家的兴奋。经过一两个小时的旅程后，女孩们有点疲惫不堪，而我们得在飞机上待上大约12个小时。我和她们聊了聊，建议她们去上个厕所并活动一下身体。随着夜色渐深，她们变得昏昏欲睡。我在空姐的帮助下给她们盖上温暖的毯子。睡了一夜好觉之后，她们感觉好多了，并期待着在另一个国家看到营地学校。

到达美国当地小学时，我们受到了主办方的热情欢迎，孩子们对异国生活充满了好奇。当我看到她们兴奋的表情时，我觉得照顾她们的辛苦工作是非常值得的。

与此同时，我也有机会体验中美两国不同的文化。更重要的是，我获得了照顾孩子的经验，这对一个老师或一个母亲来说是非常重要的。

那次旅行是我第一次去美国。我参观了美国的一些景点，比如自由女神像，我还去了纽约和费城。我想把这次旅行推荐给每个人，因为这真的是一次很棒的经历。

➤重点词汇及短语

1. gain [geɪn] *vt.* 获得；赢得；博得；取得

2. camp [kæmp] *n.* 度假营

3. organizer [ˈɔːɡənaɪzə(r)] *n.* 组织者

4. local [ˈləʊkl] *adj.* 地方的；当地的；本地的

5. elementary [ˌelɪˈmentri] *adj.* 初级的；基础的

6. nervous [ˈnɜːvəs] *adj.* 焦虑的；担忧的；易紧张焦虑的

7. delicious [dɪˈlɪʃəs] *adj.* 美味的；可口的；芬芳的

8. excitement [ɪkˈsaɪtmənt] *n.* 激动；兴奋；刺激

9. exhausted [ɪɡˈzɔːstɪd] *adj.* 筋疲力尽的；疲惫不堪的

10. drowsy [ˈdraʊzi] *adj.* 困倦的；昏昏欲睡的

11. stewardess [ˌstjuːəˈdes] *n.* （飞机上的）女乘务员；空中小姐

12. blanket [ˈblæŋkɪt] *n.* 毯子；毛毯

13. greet [griːt] *vt.* 和（某人）打招呼（或问好）；欢迎；迎接

14. warmly [wɔːmlɪ] *adv.* 亲切地；热烈地；热心地

15. recommend [ˌrekəˈmend] *vt.* 推荐；举荐；介绍

16. care for 照料；照顾

➤重点句型

1. spend sth. on... 在……方面花费……

　　例：I could spend each day gorging on chocolate.

　　　　我可以将每一天都花在狂吃巧克力上。

2. be curious about 对……感到好奇

　　例：Children tend to be curious about things they see.

　　　　儿童往往会对他们所看到的事物感到好奇。

3. have the opportunity to do... 有机会做……

　　例：And even if they do learn a second language at school, they rarely have the opportunity to practice it, unfortunately.

　　　　不幸的是，即使他们在上学时学了第二语言，也鲜有机会在生活中得到运用。

4.

　　题目翻译：

你应该在这项任务上花费大约30分钟。

你们学校的校刊将出版特刊，欢迎学生在新学年返校。你被要求写一篇文章，说明设定学习目标的重要性。

在你的文章中，你应该说明：

• 制定学习目标的重要性
• 学生应设定何种目标
• 学生可以如何获得实现目标所需的支持

以及其他你认为重要的点。

至少写180个单词。

参考范文：

I am writing this article to express my opinion on what learning goals students should set for the new school year and the importance of setting learning goals.

Learning goals are essential for students as they enter the new school year. The goals are the navigational equivalent of a lighthouse, guiding us in a clear direction so that we will have the enthusiasm to study hard. When we achieve our goals, we feel a sense of accomplishment. Without a learning objective, you will not be able to measure your progress. Establishing learning goals is also conducive to the formation of good learning habits, which can rapidly improve academic performance.

For the new school year, students can set goals as follows: First, we should correct our learning attitude by listening carefully in class and finishing homework carefully after class. Secondly, we should improve our academic performance by small steps. Finally, take a hard look at yourself and reduce the number of frivolous mistakes.

If there are any questions that need to be addressed along the way to your goal, please contact the learning commissary in your class. If they cannot resolve the problem, send an e-mail to the teacher's e-mail address and the teacher will get back to you the next day.

范文翻译：

我写这篇文章是为了表达我对新学年学生应该设定什么学习目标和设定学习目标的重要性的看法。

对于进入新学年的学生来说，学习目标至关重要。它们是航海中的灯塔，指引着我们朝着明确的方向前进，使我们有努力学习的热情。当我们实现目标时，我们会有成就感。没有学习目标，你就无法衡量自己的进步。学习目标的确立也有利于形成良好的学习习惯，可以迅速提高学习成绩。

对于新学年，学生可以设定以下目标：首先，我们应该纠正我们的学习态度，上课认真听讲，课后认真完成作业。其次，我们应该一步步地提高我们的学习成绩。最后，认真审视自己，减少不必要的错误。

如果在实现目标的过程中有任何需要解决的问题，请联系你所在班级的学习委员。如果他们不能解决问题，向老师的电子邮件地址发送电子邮件，老师会在第二天给你回复。

➤ 重点词汇及短语

---

1. express [ɪkˈspres] *vt.* 表示；表达；表露

2. importance [ɪmˈpɔːtns] *n.* 重要性；重要；重大

3. navigational [ˌnævɪˈɡeɪʃənl] *adj.* 航行的，航海的

4. equivalent [ɪˈkwɪvələnt] *n.* 等同物；对应物

5. lighthouse [ˈlaɪthaʊs] *n.* 灯塔

6. enthusiasm [ɪnˈθjuːziæzəm] *n.* 热情；热心；热忱

7. achieve [əˈtʃiːv] *vt.* 实现，达到；完成

8. objective [əbˈdʒektɪv] *n.* 目标；目的

9. formation [fɔːˈmeɪʃn] *n.* 形成；构成

10. rapidly [ˈræpɪdlɪ] *adv.* 快速地，迅速地

11. academic [ˌækəˈdemɪk] *adj.* 学业的，教学的，学术的

12. attitude [ˈætɪtjuːd] *n.* 态度，看法

13. reduce [rɪˈdjuːs] *vt.* 减少，缩小

14. frivolous [ˈfrɪvələs] *adj.* 无价值的，毫无意义的

15. commissary [ˈkɒmɪsəri] *n.* 代表，委员

16. sense of accomplishment 成就感

➤ 重点句型

1. opinion on... 对……的意见

   例：Everyone had an opinion on the subject.

   大家对这个问题都有自己的看法。

2. be essential for... 对……是必不可少的

   例：Breathable and waterproof clothing is essential for most outdoor sports.

   大多数户外运动衣服必须透气且防水。

3. be conducive to 有助于……

   例：We believe personal contact will be conducive to the promotion of better understanding.

   我们相信面对面接触将有助于促进更好的了解。

Day 9 考前冲刺篇

Part 1

题目翻译:

你应该在这项任务上花费大约15分钟。

你的狗不见了。你想通知你所有的邻居。

给他们发一封邮件,在邮件中你应该:

- 解释情况

- 对狗进行描述

- 告诉他们可以做些什么来提供帮助

至少写50个单词。

参考范文:

Dear neighbors,

Betty has not got back home for 24 hours and it's the first time something like this happens. If you don't know her, she's quite small with short and black hair, and is wearing a pink collar. Please find a picture attached. May I ask you to look around and to call me if you see her? My phone number is 7748 1582.

Thank you for your help.

Amelia

范文翻译：

亲爱的邻居：

贝蒂已经24小时没有回家了，这是第一次发生这样的事情。如果你不认识它，我可以告诉你，它身材娇小，黑色短毛，戴着粉红色的项圈。请查收附件中的图片。我请求你四处看看，如果你看到它就给我打电话，好吗？我的电话号码是7748 1582。

谢谢你的帮助。

阿米莉亚

➢ 重点词汇及短语

---

1. neighbor [ˈneɪbə] *n.* 邻居，邻国

2. pink [pɪŋk] *adj.* 粉红色的

3. collar [ˈkɒlə（r）] *n.* 衣领；（动物）颈圈；箍

4. attached [əˈtætʃt] *adj.* 附加的，附属的

5. look around 到处寻找；搜寻

➢ 重点句型

1. may I ask you to... 可以请你……吗？

    例：Mr Green, may I ask you to speak about student accommodation?
    格林先生，可以请你谈一谈学生宿舍的问题吗？

Part 2

题目翻译：

你应该在这项任务上花费大约30分钟。

你在你的大学网站上看到了这个通知。

> 给我们写一篇评论，评论你用来学习的一个网站！
>
> 告诉我们一个你用来学习的网站。它有什么好处？还有改进的地方吗？你会把网站推荐给谁？

写一篇关于你用来学习的网站的评论。

评论内容包括：

• 你为什么喜欢这个网站

• 如何让网站变得更好

• 你会把网站推荐给谁

以及其他你认为重要的点。

至少写180个单词。

参考范文：

In this review, I will explain a useful website I have used for my studies. I will explain its merits, as well as those of which it should be improved.

As an English major, a good English dictionary is essential in my studies. After many attempts, I found the website of www.youdao.com, an online dictionary. The website has a number of features. In addition to its fundamental function of explaining words, it provides many examples of the correct usage of words. Also, it provides contractions of some words with similar meanings, which is very helpful for English learners. On the other hand, it offers dictionary services in many languages, such as Chinese, Japanese, Spanish and German.

With a wide range of examples, this site already covers many examples from other sites. However, there are a few glitches in the examples that can cause confusion for beginners. I therefore recommend a serious examination of the examples in the collection from other sites.

With its large capacity in terms of the number of words and detailed explanations in terms of the word usage, I would recommend this site to beginners in language learning. Additionally, with its application of translation from photos, which is very convenient for employees who are confronted with unfamiliar words on the job, I would recommend this site to employees who need to process work in different languages.

From my experience, I think www.youdao.com is a very useful site and hope it can rectify its shortcomings and become a useful language learning tool for more and more people.

范文翻译：

在这篇评论中，我将说明一个我在学习中使用过的实用网站。我将说明它的优点，以及它应该改进的地方。

作为一名英语专业的学生，一个好的英语词典对我的学习是必不可少的。经过多次尝试，我找到了 www.youdao.com 的网站，这是一个在线词典。这个网站有很多特色。除了解释单词的基本功能外，它还提供了许多例子来说明单词正确用法。此外，它还提供一些含义相似的单词的缩略形式，这对英语学习者很有帮助。另一方面，它提供多种语言的词典服务，如汉语、日语、西班牙语和德语。

由于提供的示例范围广泛，本网站已经涵盖了其他网站的许多示例。但是，示例中有一些小差错可能会使初学者感到困惑。因此，我建议认真检查从其他网站收集的示例。

网站拥有庞大的词汇量和详细的词汇用法解释，我会向语言学习初学者推荐这个网站。此外，它应用了照片翻译功能，对于在工作中遇到陌生单词的员工来说非常方便，我会把这个网站推荐给需要处理不同语言工作的员工。

从我的经验来看，我认为 www.youdao.com 是一个非常实用的网站，希望它能纠正缺点，成为越来越多人们学习语言的实用工具。

➤重点词汇及短语

1. website ['websaɪt] *n.* 网站

2. explain [ɪk'spleɪn] *vt.* 解释；说明；阐明

3. merit ['merɪt] *n.* 优点；美德；价值

4. major ['meɪdʒə(r)] *n.* 主修学生；专业

5. dictionary ['dɪkʃənəri] *n.* 词典；字典；辞书

6. essential [ɪ'senʃl] *adj.* 完全必要的；必不可少的；极其重要的

7. attempt [ə'tempt] *n.* 企图；试图；尝试

8. fundamental [ˌfʌndə'mentl] *adj.* 基础的；基本的

9. example [ɪg'zɑːmpl] *n.* 实例；例证；例子

10. contraction [kən'trækʃn] *n.* 词的缩约形式

11. Spanish ['spænɪʃ] *n.* 西班牙语；西班牙人

12. glitch [glɪtʃ] *n.* 小过失，差错

13. confusion [kən'fjuːʒn] *n.* 不确定；困惑

14. examination [ɪgˌzæmɪ'neɪʃn] *n.* 审查，考察；检查

15. collection [kə'lekʃn] *n.* 收集；聚集

16. capacity [kə'pæsəti] *n.* 容量；容积；容纳能力

17. application [ˌæplɪ'keɪʃn] *n.* 运用；生效

18. process ['prəʊses] *vt.* 审阅，审核，处理（文件、请求等）

19. a wide range of 大范围的；许多各种不同的

20. in terms of 就……而言；在……方面

➤重点句型

1. be convenient for 方便……；便于……

例：When will it be convenient for you to come?

什么时候对你来说最方便？

2. be confronted with... 面临……；面对……

例：I did not want to be confronted with that situation.

我不想面对那种情况。

全真模拟题二

Part 1

题目翻译：

你应该在这项任务上花费大约15分钟。

您收到了这封来自您购物的网上商店的电子邮件。

亲爱的客户，

感谢您的订单。

我们的送货司机到达您附近时会和您联系。

您说过最好是在早上送货。但是我们知道大家都很忙，所以如果您不在家，您能告诉我们司机可以把包裹放在哪里吗？

祝好，

凯莉

销售团队

给凯莉写一封电子邮件：

· 告诉对方你早上什么时候可以接收快递

· 描述一下如果你外出，送货司机可以把包裹放在什么地方

· 说明送货司机可以联系到你的最佳方式。

至少写50个单词。

参考范文：

Dear Kelly,

Very glad to receive your email!

As you mentioned in your email, many people are busy in the morning. I have to explain that my normal working hours are from 4 p.m. to 12 p.m. at midnight, so I am free in the morning. And I can take delivery in the morning.

If the delivery driver is busy and I am out of the house, the delivery driver can drop off the items at Lawson Convenience Store at the community gate. Please keep the goods in good order and tell the staff at the store that I will take the goods back as soon as possible.

Most of the time, I will be at home to receive the goods. If I am out and the item is placed at Lawson Convenience Store, please tell the delivery driver to call me at the phone number on the order or another number 13741520123. Thanks.

Best wishes!
Daniel

范文翻译：

亲爱的凯莉：

很高兴收到您的电子邮件！

正如您在电子邮件中提到的，许多人早上都很忙。我必须说明一下我的正常工作时间是从下午4点到午夜12点，所以我早上有空。我可以在早上收货。

如果送货司机很忙而送货时我不在家，那么送货司机可以把货物放在小区门口的罗森便利店。请把货物整理好，并告诉店员我将尽快取回货物。

大多数时候，我会在家接收货物。如果我不在，并且货物放在了罗森便利店，请告诉送货司机打订单上的电话号码或另外一个号码13741520123告诉我一下。谢谢。

祝好！

丹尼尔

➤重点词汇及短语

---

1. delivery [dɪˈlɪvəri] *n.* 递送（商品）

2. contact [ˈkɒntækt] *vt.* 联系，联络（如用电话或信件）

3. package [ˈpækɪdʒ] *n.* 包裹；包装盒

4. mention [ˈmenʃn] *vt.* 提到；写到；说到

5. normal [ˈnɔːml] *adj.* 典型的；正常的；一般的

6. midnight [ˈmɪdnaɪt] *n.* 午夜；子夜

7. convenience [kənˈviːniəns] *n.* 方便；适宜；便利

8. community [kəˈmjuːnəti] *n.* 社区；社会

9. staff [stɑːf] *n.* 全体职工（或雇员）

10. in good order 有条不紊，整齐，情况正常

➤重点句型

1. be available to do 可以做……

　　例：When would you be available to start working here?

　　　　你什么时候可以开始来这边上班？

Part 2

题目翻译：

> 你应该在这项任务上花费大约30分钟。
>
> 你居住的城镇有一个网站，你可以在上面讨论当地的问题。你最近参观了一个新的休闲中心，其广告如下。
>
> 为网站写一篇评论。
> 在你的评论中提及以下内容：
> * 到休闲中心的交通情况
> * 休闲中心内的设备和设施
> * 什么人群适合去休闲中心
> 以及其他你认为重要的点。
>
> 至少写180个单词。

> 常青藤休闲中心
>
> 欢迎来我们的现代休闲中心进行免费体验。这里交通便利，距离市中心不到一英里。
>
> 在这里您可以体验到最新的健身器材，并可以在我们奥林匹克规格的滑冰场滑冰。如果您在锻炼之后感到饥饿，没有问题，我们的咖啡馆和餐厅提供各种口味的食物。休闲中心的工作人员具有丰富的经验，可以解答您所有关于健康的问题。

参考范文：

I would highly recommend people who want to get fit to go to the Ivy Vine Leisure Centre, which is not only convenient but also has a lot of fitness and recreation facilities.

The leisure centre is located very close to the city centre, which is less than a mile away. People can walk, take buses or drive, and there are many parking spaces in the leisure center, which is convenient for people who drive. The facilities in the leisure center are very modern, and the gym is equipped with the latest fitness equipment, which can fully mobilize people's desire to exercise.

In addition to fitness equipment, the leisure center also has various amusement facilities and children's parks, where parents can take their children with them. While adults work out, children can have fun. In addition, the leisure center has a big skating rink, where coaches can teach people how to skate, and people who want to practice skating can practice there.

After a lot of exercise, hungry people can refuel at the cafes and restaurants in the leisure center. People can have a nice cup of coffee, a snack or even a meal from the regular menu. With a wide variety of dishes on offer, even people with special dietary requirements can find food here to their satisfaction.

All in all, if you want to improve your physical fitness, or just want to meet friends for coffee or a meal, the Ivy Vine Leisure Centre is a good choice. Go and experience it!

范文翻译：

> 我强烈推荐想要健身的人们去常春藤休闲中心，这里不仅交通方便还有很多健身及游乐设施。
>
> 休闲中心离市中心非常近，距离不到一英里，人们可以步行过来，也可以乘坐公共汽车或开车过来，休闲中心有很多停车位，方便开车过来的人们。休闲中心内的设施很现代，健身房内配备最新式的健身器材，能充分调动人们锻炼身体的欲望。
>
> 休闲中心除了有健身器材外，还有各种游乐设施和儿童乐园，家长可以带孩子一起前往。在大人健身的同时，孩子可以快乐地玩耍。此外，休闲中心还有一个很大的溜冰场，教练可以教人们如何滑冰，想要练习溜冰的人们可以在那里练习。
>
> 在经过了大量运动之后，饥饿的人们可以在休闲中心的咖啡馆和餐厅补充点能量。人们可以喝杯可口的咖啡，吃点小吃，甚至吃上日常菜单上的一顿饭。这里提供的菜品种类繁多，即使有特殊饮食要求的人们也可以在这里找到令自己满意的食物。
>
> 总而言之，如果你想改善锻炼身体，或者只是想和朋友一起喝杯咖啡或吃顿饭，常春藤休闲中心是一个不错的选择。赶紧去体验一下吧！

➢ 重点词汇及短语

1. leisure ['leʒə(r)] *n.* 闲暇；空闲；休闲

2. convenient [kən'viːniənt] *adj.* 便利的；方便的

3. recreation [ˌriːkri'eɪʃn] *n.* 娱乐；消遣

4. facility [fə'sɪləti] *n.* 设施；设备

5. modern ['mɒdn] *adj.* 时新的；现代化的；最新的

6. gym [dʒɪm] *n.* 健身房；体育馆

7. latest ['leɪtɪst] *adj.* 最近的；最新的

8. mobilize ['məʊbəlaɪz] *vt.* 调动；动员；组织

9. desire [dɪ'zaɪə(r)] *n.* 愿望；欲望；渴望

10. amusement [ə'mjuːzmənt] *n.* 娱乐活动；游戏

11. adult ['ædʌlt] *n.* 成年人

12. rink [rɪŋk] *n.* 溜冰场；冰球场

13. coach [kəʊtʃ] *n.* （体育运动的）教练

14. refuel [ˌriː'fjuːəl] *vi.* （给）加油，加燃料

15. cafe ['kæfeɪ] *n.* 咖啡馆，小餐馆

16. snack [snæk] *n.* 快餐，点心

17. menu ['menjuː] *n.* 菜单

18. special ['speʃl] *adj.* 特殊的；特别的；不寻常的；不一般的

19. dietary ['daɪətəri] *adj.* 饮食的；膳食中的

20. satisfaction [ˌsætɪs'fækʃn] *n.* 满足；满意；欣慰

21. all in all 总的来说，大体而言；总而言之

➢ 重点句型

1. would highly recommend 强烈推荐

　　例：I would highly recommend this product to all parents.
　　　　我强烈推荐所有的父母都使用这款产品！

2. be located... 位于；坐落于……

　　例：Our new office will be located in the city.
　　　　我们的新办公室将设在这个城市里。

3. be equipped with... 配备有……

　　例：Our factory is equipped with modern machines.
　　　　我们工厂配备了现代化的机器。